GAR14-1

ALSO BY HARRY ADDISON

Write That Down For Me Daddy, 1974

RFD #3

Harry Addison

PELICAN PUBLISHING COMPANY
GRETNA 1977

Library of Congress Cataloging in Publication Data

Addison, Harry.
    RFD 3.

    I. Title.
PS3551.D398R14   818'.5'407   77-23069
ISBN 0-88289-161-8

Manufactured in the United States of America
Designed by Oscar Richard
Published by Pelican Publishing Company, Inc.
630 Burmaster Street, Gretna, Louisiana 70053

In memory of Mama and Papa
and all the other fine folks
who lived in Swartz.

ROUTE 3, MONROE

Mama never could say we lived at Swartz . . . it was a stigma to her. She always said we lived at Route 3, Monroe. I guess it was the memory of her mother telling them they came from "royalty." I never cared where I was from, I was so glad to be where I was at.

Mama was a prideful woman, especially about her cooking. She was something in the kitchen and, even during the Depression, could fair more bake a cake.

We were packing food for the All-Day-Singing and-Dinner-on-the-Ground-Home-Demonstration-Annual-Picnic at McGuire's Park in West Monroe and I was ready. There just never was anything like it. Everybody who thought they could cook would be there, and, in the lean years, even the uppity could stir a pot.

We had the old Model T stuffed with every kind of goody you could can or put in a fruit jar, and Papa was as excited as the rest of us. Mama was like an old hen, clucking around her biddies as she rounded up her arts. Then off we clattered.

I could hardly wait to get a dipper in that No. 3 tub of lemonade. It was at one of these outings that I discovered a great phenomenon—a nine-year-old could hold four gallons of anything made cold with "store-bought" ice.

We fell out of the fliver . . . having fun, running, whooping, hollering, working up a blue ribbon thirst. Seemed like we hardly had our feet on the ground when they called us to eat. Never was a time I could eat more.

We always got home from these festivities after dark and cows had to be milked, hogs slopped, eggs gathered and everybody tuckered out, dirty, sweaty, sticky, smelly and the cows almost as aggravated about the hour as we were. It didn't make Papa any difference if every crock in the house was full of milk . . . we couldn't turn the calves in because the cows wouldn't let the milk down for us anymore if we did. So I'd go out there in the dark and cuss the cows, but I

9

knew God didn't hold that against a tired country boy.

I stripped the cows and then turned in the bellering calves and started for the house. The hogs were telling Papa I hadn't fed them, so I set the milk pail high on a shelf in the feed house to keep the cat from getting in it. Then I picked up the soured bran mix and poured it on the upturned snouts of the shoats standing in the trough—half on them and half on my brogans. I had to mix another batch of bran so it would be soured for morning, but I couldn't find the stirring paddle in the dark, so I just dug in above my elbow and swirled. When I got to the house, Mama took one look at my arm and screamed. With all that bran clinging to it, it looked like I had the Far Eastern Itch. Papa just grinned and rinsed me off. He'd been in the bucket before.

After a hot bath, I fell across the bed. This would be another night I would not finish my conversation with God.

✝   ✝   ✝

Being the youngest boy, I wore a lot of hand-me-downs and now that my son is outgrowing me—I wear a lot of "hand-me-ups."

✝   ✝   ✝

Raising children becomes worthwhile when they get enough sense to realize we've got enough sense to raise them.

Holding Hands

I love you with so much of me
I let my mind run at ease.
With slackened reins it runs

through the green meadow,
over mountain peaks covered with snow,
through cold, swift-running brooks
that numb your feet,
across rocky slopes with ringing hooves.

Yet it never runs alone,
for it always runs with you.

✝   ✝   ✝

Many times, just toeing the line beats going an extra mile.

✝   ✝   ✝

When mini-dresses are worn, it's easy to see what kind of limb a girl can get herself out on.

✝   ✝   ✝

My romance with the English language is like trying to imitate a bird. I can hop around on the ground, but I've never been able to fly.

✝   ✝   ✝

The greatest fool in society's employ is the one who mistakes knuckling under for kindness. In the final hour, he is the first one to fall.

Chivalry is not dead—it's just getting to be an old man.

†　　　　†　　　　†

Prejudice is a polluted stream eroding away trust among mankind.

†　　　　†　　　　†

One of the most expensive things in life is very easy to acquire . . . a taste for luxurious living.

†　　　　†　　　　†

I suppose the reason I've never feared losing my employ is that I know I am not indispensible—but neither are those who employ me.

†　　　　†　　　　†

The tongues of some men should be like those in their shoes—laced in public and loosed only at the end of day.

†　　　　†　　　　†

I have reached the age where a peaceful plateau of tranquillity is achieved simply by understanding my teenagers and being understood by them.

†　　　　†　　　　†

Mama would have been a good con man. All during the Depression, she had us kids believing tripe was deep-sea fish.

†　　　　†　　　　†

Men should never try to outsmart women; after all, only the first woman came from man, after which they reversed the procedure.

†　　　　†　　　　†

My dad used to say, "The neck of the chicken is my favorite piece." What he really meant was, "I love you more than I love me, so you eat the pully bone."

†　　　　†　　　　†

There was one thing I enjoyed during the Depression that all the money in the world cannot buy for me now . . . YOUTH.

A WHEELBARROW FULL OF BOOZE

Cliff never could whisper. He'd just change the pitch of his voice, not the volume. So we'd make him write all secret messages in the dust 'cause you could hear him clean out to the barn.

One evening at twilight, as we were finishing up a game of tin can shinny, we heard him come a-running, whispering at the top of his lungs, "Y'all come on down heah. Old Man Carlow is drunker 'n Cooter Brown and layin' out in the middle of the gravel road!!"

We called the game and ran 'cause Old Man Carlow was an artist of alcohol. Even his hair got soused. This was gonna be a real good ending for a hot summer day.

Me 'n Sid 'n Robert 'n Cliff tried to pick him up, but he was so limber he'd just flop out somewhere else and moan—Ooooooo me, oooooooh me." "Do you feel all right, Mr. Carlow?" "Boys, I ain't never felt better in my whole life. Oooooooh me."

He made drunk sound so good it got you to wondering if the preacher was on the level when he told you how evil it was. Well, Old Man Carlow was a disciple of the devil tonight if the parson was right.

We tried dragging him, but his head was bouncing so we didn't figger he was pleasured by our samaritanism. Cliff thought of a great conveyance and, with a whoop, disappeared into the night. In no time at all he was back with an old wooden wheelbarrow, whereupon we rolled and tugged 'til we got him belly up in the thing. Well, everything 'cept his arms 'n hands which drug to each side as we rolled him toward his house. Better his hands than his head!

We drug him up on his porch and set him up in his rocker. Next morning when he woke, he swore he was gonna quit drinking 'cause he knew he had fought a wild beast and didn't even remember what it was!

"Well, looka' heah! You can tell I did, cause my hands is still a'bleedin'."

We never did tell him he'd lost to a gravel road and a wheelbarrow. I think he knew, though, 'cause Cliff had been whispering it around the quarters.

Coon Shine

Love
Is remembering
When others forget -----------
Love
Is an earth's turn
From a golden sunset -----------
Love
Is a willow
Remembered in dreams ------------
Love
Is a sandbar
By a quiet flowing stream ------------
Love
Of you
Is a part
Of me
Of the stream
Of the dream
And our willow tree -----------

LET THE WIND WHISTLE

Newty 'n Lloyd were standing by the cattle gap at the railroad crossing, looking at something brassy.

Me 'n Calvin 'n Howard had been over behind the carbon plant sniping some old tin for the roof of our clubhouse. It'd take a gallon of hot tar per sheet to stop up all the nail holes, but we didn't care.

"Hey! Whatcha got there?" Calvin hollered.

"We found us a whistle. I bet it come off a train or somethin'," Newty decided. "Let's build us a steam boiler and make it moan. I bet we could scare hell outa' folks when they go over the crossing."

We found us a fifty-five gallon drum that still had the top and bottom and didn't leak. We filled it about one-fourth full with water, then unscrewed the smaller bung and replaced it with the whistle.

"Tie this rope to that thing and hang it on a limb so it won't burn. That's what makes it work," somebody advised.

Man, it was hot. We had the fire dancing around the bottom of our homemade boiler and we could hear the water stirring, but we never could get up any steam.

The barrel needed to be up off the ground so the heat could get under the water. We broke up in teams to scout for a suitable rack to support our project. When we all reassembled, it looked like a Junkmen's Convention down on Stubb's Vinson Road.

We all decided on a set of old bedsprings—the kind with cone-shaped coils. It was just right . . . high enough to let the fire spread evenly across the bottom of the barrel. We threw pine knots, old tires, and anything else we could get to burn around the bottom of our boiler. We were all sweating 'n laughing, waiting for the first head of steam and an unsuspecting driver.

Someone suggested we all go to the Perkins' pump for a cool drink and let the fire do its duty. "Last one there's a double dog ugly hog." The boiler brigade was off in a flash—a sweaty, running wad of noise.

"Last one there's gotta pump, last one's gotta pump!" I was doing fine 'til my head outran my feet and I got to pump.

All of us nearly foundered ourselves 'n had one more drink, then we settled back to let our stomachs gurgle.

We were about ready to go back to our steamer when the countryside was obliged with a deafening roar that shook houses and cracked windows, caused hens to quit laying and dried up cows. A cloud of steam and black smoke marked the untimely end of our project. We ran pell mell to the site and found a hole in the ground. No barrel, no whistle . . . the coils were all we ever found. They hung from the pines as though the trees had just had their hair rolled.

Nevertheless, we scared hell out of somebody cause old Sam's Model T truck was across the ditch and still running, butting a sapling and Sam long gone. He finally came back next day, but his hair was gray.

✝   ✝   ✝

Remembering the good things in life is like carrying a jack in your car. You don't need it all the time, but it sure gives you a lift when you do.

✝   ✝   ✝

A smile doesn't always cure ugly . . . but it sure keeps it from spreading.

✝   ✝   ✝

If we were all born blind, white would not be white, black would not be black, red would not be red, yellow would not be yellow, but a man would still be a man.

✝   ✝   ✝

To be in love with a dream is almost as warm as dreaming of the one you love.

Usually the best mechanism of escape from a boring situation is to let the other fellow say something.

✝   ✝   ✝

I'm at the age where just getting over getting up is getting me down.

✝   ✝   ✝

Earning a college degree may not make you a better prospect, but it seems to make your prospects better.

✝   ✝   ✝

The clearest path may not be the surest footing and the most elegant entry may not mean a waiting welcome.

✝   ✝   ✝

I do not wish my son to follow in my footsteps. It would only cause him to bog down sooner.

✝   ✝   ✝

I don't believe hard work is the only requisite to great wealth, for I have never been acquainted with a millionaire mule. However I must admit to fellowship with some rich jackasses.

✝   ✝   ✝

The line we're holding on higher prices will most likely be the rope that hangs us.

✝   ✝   ✝

I knew a fellow who was so proud he told the truth all the time, he'd sometimes lie about it just to prove it.

✝   ✝   ✝

Education is the great transformer. It can turn a sharecropper's son into a respected surgeon and a miner's child into a revered theologian. Therefore, if a man desires a higher station in life, tickets can be bought at the schoolhouse.

17

BLACKIE'S LAST LOOK

There were three of us boys and I was the youngest. The oldest I called "Big Brother," and the other I dubbed "Little Brother," and they obliged me by referring to me as the "Old Man." I suppose it was because, as I walked, I would cross my hands behind my back as the elderly have a habit of doing.

The youngest or smallest seem to be imparted by nature with the ability to pit their opponents' cleverness back upon them—not unlike holding a wasp with a stick until it stings itself to death.

My fat brother and I slept in the same bed and he could never understand why I always let him beat me to bed. He'd hit the old feather mattress and roll and all the stuffing would move to the other side like chaff before the wind. I'd be ready and would always sleep high on the down side.

Sleep came quickly that night and the next voice I heard was Papa's . . . seemed like I never even closed my eyes.

"Boys! Boys!" Slowly the sound penetrated our slumber. "Yes sir," we all chorused.

"Get up and come help me."

"What's the matter, Papa?"

"Old Blackie didn't come up this morning. Come on."

Blackie was the best Holstein, best cow we ever owned. She seemed to love us and we sure loved her. She sustained us. Every meal centered around her gifts—butter, milk, cream, buttermilk for biscuits, clabber. Papa always liked clabber, 'specially with syrup stirred in it. He could sure make it sound good when he slurped it down.

"Let's go, boys." We heard the anxiety in his voice so we made haste and met Papa at the cow lot.

School was just gonna have to wait. We had to find Blackie if she was sick. She couldn't last long . . . the snow was falling fast and the weather was fierce. The wind was sharp on every side and cut through worn breeches like a ra-

18

zor. I was already calling her before I left the gate. "Soo, Cow, Soo . . . Sooo-oo-oo, Cow." If Blackie could hear me, she'd come.

I headed toward the carbon plant. All the animals liked to hang around the hot houses where the carbon was formed. Sure cut the cold in quarters and rounded off the hurt. She wasn't there, so I turned east along the creek, crossed the gravel road, and struck out for the cedars. For no known reason, I started back toward home. "Soo Cow, Soo!"

I'll never know whether I felt or heard the sound. I ran up in the pine grove and there she was, trying to get up. I tried to soothe her and leave her with some sort of courage, then lit out like a banshee, hollering for Papa.

The school bus had long since left the Addisons.

Papa took over operations and began giving out directions. "Ed, you get the block and tackle, the axe, and croacker sacks. Little Brother, you get the rope and coal oil. Show Ed where she is, Old Man, and you all get a fire started. We got to get her on her feet, boys, or she'll die."

We cut poles and lashed them to the trees around her, fashioned a sling under her belly to which we attached a ring, ran a rope through the ring and attached it to the hook on the block and tackle and slowly raised her to a standing position. We made a windbreak out of our old tarp on the north side of Blackie and built up a fire. She looked at us with those big, round eyes and thanked us as only an animal can. Nobody knew what was wrong with her . . . she just couldn't stand.

I set a foot tub of fresh drawn water where she could drink, but she wouldn't even try.

The weather got colder and we kept fighting it and on the morning of the third day, it was a wasp with a cold stinger. I fell out of bed and made for old Blackie. I wanted to build up her fire so she wouldn't get cold while I was at school.

I couldn't see any steam coming out of her snoot and ran faster. When I got up alongside her, the water was frozen solid in the tub and her head was stiff to her side, looking toward the house. The moisture was frozen in her nose.

Old Blackie would never feel the cold again. I turned and the tears stung my eyes. I walked slowly back to the house. Papa wouldn't look at me. Mama couldn't talk either. They didn't tell me to catch the bus, for I had learned a lesson that day they would not teach in school.

Marathon Parade

Night appears
in black silken gown
with starlike sequins
everywhere . . .

Followed by
her blue-eyed escort,
a broad-shouldered lad
with flaming hair . . .

They swirl and whirl
around the world
with laughter or
with crying . . .

bringing news of someone's
borning and other times a
dying . . .

On and on and on they march
this marathon parade,
endlessly in love
or an endless charade . . .

In the art of being versatile, two of the most difficult virtues to acquire are for the young to teach change without affronting and the old to learn it without prejudice.

† † †

I began to enjoy life much more when I became aware that it is a privilege to live on earth and no one man or race has the franchise.

† † †

Everytime I drink too much, it lowers my resistance and the next morning I have an alcoholic virus.

† † †

To be thought a fool by your enemy is endurable, but to be called a dolt by those who are supposed to love you is a heavy load.

† † †

Each day history repeats itself, I am more convinced of reincarnation. Man simply could not have become so stupid in one lifetime.

On Politics

When a politician proclaims he is going to return honesty to government, it is almost a certainty he was guilty of its disappearance in the first place.

† † †

Our welfare program is like a woman who needs a girdle. We, too, have let things get out of shape before trying to control the figure.

† † †

To know the difference between growth and inflation takes an astute mind. Even more rare is one that encourages the first and controls the other.

† † †

If you have a skeleton in your closet and run for political office, you can be sure someone will make some bones about it!

† † †

Sometimes, progress unwittingly makes the witless rich, for at times a super highway will locate a cloverleaf on a failure's forty, bringing wealth unearned except by fate and paid by others' taxes.

† † †

If actions speak louder than words, Congress must be filled with deaf mutes.

† † †

Trouble with charity today is there's more folks wanting to draw relief than to give it.

† † †

When a politician introduces a law with teeth in it, it usually turns out to be a new tax bite.

Politics has proved the highest up can be the lowest down.

✝ ✝ ✝

It's hard to change horses in the middle of the stream without getting your feet wet.

✝ ✝ ✝

If it were possible to recapture all the hot air from one political campaign, we could warm everyone in America for the next two winters and make nine out of ten citizens hot under the collar for a similar length of time.

✝ ✝ ✝

The Government has changed time and dates so often, we'll soon be giving dyed turkey eggs for Christmas.

✝ ✝ ✝

If the tears from those who cry for higher wages were turned to sweat, they'd be worth their salt!

✝ ✝ ✝

Christians are taught to turn the other cheek, but politicians want us to turn our heads.

✝ ✝ ✝

Watergate has introduced a new type tape that measures to what length a politician will go.

✝ ✝ ✝

If we are living in a free enterprise society, I'd hate to live in a cost-plus community.

✝ ✝ ✝

The trouble with Washington today is the Supreme Court is so liberal, politicians have started operating out in the open.

23

California is noted for its citrus groves and I'll concede they have famous fruits, but people in Washington, D. C. can boast the most prolific nut crop in the world.

† † †

The Welfare Program was designed to help the unfortunate overcome a temporary setback. Instead, it has become a pension for the poor.

† † †

The trouble with politics today is that we usually elect the most evil of the two lessers.

† † †

If the government were as frugal with the money they take from me as I have to be with what I have left, neither of us would have to worry over new taxes.

† † †

Politicians claim bussing school children will achieve racial balance. That makes about as much sense as the way they balance everything else in Washington, D. C.

† † †

The squeeze taxpayers are caught in with "give away programs" should be referred to as "Foreign Ade."

† † †

When man breaks a law, he is chipping away the mortar that holds his society together.

† † †

I believe bussing is the correct answer to better education . . . except it should be quality teachers who are bussed to the students.

† † †

The brilliant wheat deals our politicians have made with Russia have caused bread to rise faster than yeast. If it keeps going up, we'll soon be putting it between slices of ham.

The energy shortage that concerns me most is my teenaged son's.

✝ ✝ ✝

There is a bit of absurdity in our government when a legislator of seventy-five can decide a citizen of sixty-five must retire.

DEER DON'T EAT CHOCOLATE BARS

The day was hot and gnats were hovering over the five-gallon crock of crushed late apples, sugar, and water that was turning to cider. We was tempted to have a taste, 'cept Mama showed up. So me 'n Sid lit out for the crossing to git up a game of deer 'n dogs if we could round up enough to play.

We soon had whooped up thirty-eight savages 'n I picked up a piece of bark and spit on one side 'n threw it up in the air 'n hollered at the same time "wet side, wet side!" When it came down, the dry side was on the ground, so I got to be the deer 'n could choose another one. So I picked Sid—"Ya'll give us a hundred count lead 'n no cheatin'."

We took off runnin'—it wouldn't take long for 'em to get to a hundred when they was countin' for a chase. We headed for the sweet gum thicket. We could make time there 'cause once we got to the top of the first gum, we could swing to the other 'n another 'n it wouldn't be long fore we'd gone across a forty, then on the last one we'd bend to the ground 'n keep a-runnin'.

We hadn't let our shirttails touch our backs since we commenced to be the deer. We cut back across the hill and up toward Springhill Cemetery. Lordy, it was hot! Sweat was runnin' out my hair 'n I had a full set of dirt beads across my guzzle bill. But we didn't stop runnin' with them dogs howlin' behind us. We doubled behind Mutt Moler's house 'n climbed an elm tree loaded with muscadines. We ate enough to harm a hog 'n shinnied down the vine 'n lit a shuck for Long Bridge Creek.

By this time, the thirty-six "dogs" had grown to forty-two, with some of 'em being real. We got to the creek where our swimmin' hole was and jumped jus' as far as we could 'n ducked under. Man, it felt good to cool off. I clawed up the muddy bank with my overalls shakin' off the water 'n my pockets slowly loosin' their contents of the creek as it strained through the heavy duck material. Sid was splashing right behind me.

Them durn dogs was hot on our tails. Well, we wasn't caught yet. Several times we thought of splittin' up but that is worse'n cheatin' at the count 'cause we was supposed to stay in sight of one 'nother.

By the high of the sun we guessed it would be 'bout two o'clock ' n wondered if the dogs had stopped for muscadines or grapes. Well, no matter, we was a long way ahead of 'em, 'cause we could jus' barely hear 'em bayin' now.

My pore ole belly was workin' on those muscadines, growlin' like I swallered a bull frog. Whew! I gotta' rest 'n I don't care if they do catch us. Old Sid was spent, too, 'n we just flopped on the ground . . . both of us sounded like we was asthmatic.

I noticed a bunch of little old holes in the ground 'n got me a pine straw 'n started pokin' down in 'em and chantin' "Doodlebug, Doodlebug, your house is on fire." I guess the straw by itself would have got an answer, but it was better if you sang "Doodlebug, Doodlebug." Soon my straw got to pushin' up and there he was . . . madder 'n the devil! By then, Old Sid was singin' to one, too.

By 'n by, the durn dogs got closer 'n sin to us. Up we jumped and lit out a-runnin'. We were about to cross the main gravel road, but had to slow 'cause a car was comin' . . . friendliest lookin' fellow who just grinned and throwed somethin' out the winder at us. We grabbed it up 'n there was two chocolate bars. We ate 'em on the run.

I heard Old Burton holler, "Yonder they go!" 'n the bayin' got louder 'cause this wuz the first time we'd been laid a eye on. I was about to be a caught deer 'cause all them muscadines, creek water, 'n candy was walkin' round in my stomach like a coon 'fore day.

Sid looked like he'd been spooked. His eyes were a foot back in his head and whiter 'n a sheet. I stumbled 'n fell 'n

27

retched. The dogs was all over us. We'd lost this race . . .
'sides, me and Sid was sick.

The other boys and the real dogs drifted off by ones 'n
twos goin' home, but me 'n Sid would spend the rest of the
day in the woods 'cause we didn't know that the friendly
feller that throwed us the candy was an Ex-Lax salesman.

Watch 'n Time

Several times today I almost called
I felt so close to you.
I wanted to hear the sounds you make
when you are happy.
I forced myself to put down the phone.
Then I played little games . . .
    "If I take a coin from my pocket
    and it's heads, I can call!
    If I lose, I'll find an
    excuse to try again."
When I won I was afraid I would bother
yet something kept compelling me to dial.
Is it because I want to be in the near of
you all the time?

I decided to wait fifteen minutes before
I called.
It was as a day in passing and I as a
child with nothing to do
I fidgeted . . . I glanced at my watch
again . . . only two minutes had passed.
I believe it's running slow
I should have it checked.

I twisted at the stem,
I leaned back in my chair,
I closed my eyes . . .
I played a game with time.
Not the now . . . time gone by . . .
I tried to imagine how you looked
at the age of ten.
You were the same in blue jeans . . .
beautiful!

I looked at my watch again—
only five minutes had passed.
I shook the stupid thing . . . it must
have stopped.
Well, something's wrong!
I dialed time . . . the monotonous voice
had the same time as my watch.
I wonder if they know their watch is
running slow?

I waited as long as I could.
Seven minutes were hours passing.
I dialed . . .
I heard your voice . . .
You were so . . . you!
I wanted to talk . . . only for a moment.
Bye . . . I love you, too.
Now what's wrong with this watch?
I talked to you only for a moment and
thirty minutes have passed.
I wish I could call you.
This watch is running slow again.

A NATURAL NURSE

The barfish were running at Riverton Locks and Dam and we were going to spend the day on the river.

Papa had packed onions, salt, pepper, lemons, meal, spuds and—just in case—corned beef. If we didn't catch any fish, he could stir up a mean pot of hash. We loaded the fishing poles and ice wrapped in newspapers, croaker sacks, and a piece of tarpaulin to have a little of it left when the day was spent.

We took off in a cloud of dust with Papa singing "Little Brown Jug." This was gonna be a good day! We stopped at Bosco and everybody got a Nehi Cola, crackers, and cheese. Then off to the dam.

The river was boiling over the locks and the fish were popping the surface, so I waded out waist-deep to meet them. Soon as my bait hit the water, it disappeared and my cork followed it under. This was one of those days when a boy forgets about school, chores, huntin', and girls. Girls! My sister was up on the bank, crying 'cause she wanted the pole I was using.

"But this un's mine!"

"Well, she's your sister and she's younger than you."

I learned another lesson in dealing with women . . . if they cry, they always win!

I got me another pole, waded back out, caught me a bar and forgot about the bawling of Betty Gene. For a sister, she was the best you could get and she was mine . . . but I sure did like that pole.

Papa whooped us up on the sandbar about two o'clock. We all set to making a fire, peeling potatoes, slicing onions, scaling fish and cutting 'em up. The grease was bubbling and I threw a kitchen match in the cauldron and it fired up at once. Time to fry fish. Everybody was hungry.

We spent many happy hours with Papa . . . singing, laughing, playing the guitar, and doing the "buck and wing" dance.

After a good nap under the willow trees, we baited up and caught half a tub of fish. We chipped ice over them and covered the whole thing with the croaker sacks and tarp, loaded the old "T," and started up the levee. Almost half-way up, the car stalled and we backed down the hill. Papa made three more runs at the levee and, each time, the old Ford's gravity feed line couldn't compete with the angle. So, he just turned the fliver around and backed up and over the top!

Once again we were headed for the house. Swartz seemed a long way at twenty-five miles an hour and we'd use the lights before we saw home.

Clouds were forming fast to the north of us and, by the time we got to Fondale, rain was an aggravation on the windshield and Betty was working the handwiper just fast enough to disturb Papa. The shower was short-lived, but it did cool off tempers and temperatures.

We came around Sicard curve and, in the twilight, we could see three cars overturned. People, chickens, eggs, buttermilk, and butter scattered all over. We pulled over and Mama jumped out crying and helping people. She had two hands full of wet cloths filled with fishy smelling ice, ministering to everybody bruised or bleeding, and wouldn't budge until the ambulance came to a gravel-grinding stop with its claxon horn still uh-ooh-gahing. Sanity was soon restored to the scene, the cars turned back on their wheels, radiators filled, chickens caught, people patched, and everybody going where they were going.

Mama settled back in the wallered out place in the front seat of the old "T" and looked up at Papa and said, "I always did want to be a nurse." He nodded and said, "I know, Mama, I know." She moved closer to him and I'd swear her face kinda' glowed in the dark.

I would live a long time before I would understand how much love a look could hold.

Turning Loose

I loved so much
I turned you loose
cutting the binds
that were no use.

I clung to you
not you to me.
Steady my hands,
I cannot see
through tears that blind
and set you free
to run your way
with head held high.
Please don't look back
for I shall cry.

Go on and run
the circle round.
When you return
it will be found
throughout your life
this you must know
I turned you loose
but couldn't let go.

To love is warm.
To be in love with those who love you is standing in the
sunshine.

†   †   †

The erosion of the mind is by far the greatest waste of
natural resources.

A LIFT FOR A BUDDY

We called our old school bus "Ironsides." The driver was a Mr. Chatmon, who dipped snuff 'n had a pile of sand between his feet for a spittoon. He'd just stir the mound with his foot so as to keep the ground turned. The bus looked like a long black barrel turned on its side and cut in half with wheels on the bottom and a flat roof supported by three uprights on each side. There were no windows 'cept the windshield and, along each side, a heavy rubberized curtain that we'd roll up in warm weather 'n try to hold down on cold, rainy days.

No one really cared about the cold or rain too much, 'cause the insides of a tomb couldn't have been any darker and anytime you stuff that many sweaty younguns in a barrel, any kinda air was welcome. Even if it was frozen. Everybody was so wadded up 'n pressed down together, a body got to know everyone else almost intimately.

One day Mr. Chatmon put my fat brother, Carl, off the bus for blowing his fist. Next morning when old Ironsides stopped to pick us up, the driver said he couldn't get on. Now Mama was a gentle woman . . . not very tall . . . but she was a mama. She stepped up to the door before the old man could close it and said, "Sir, I think you have accused my son unjustly." Whereupon Mr. Chatmon was quick to offer his authority by saying, "Now Mrs. Addison, I know your boy is guilty 'n I don't want no trouble, so I sez he don't ride for a week 'n that's final." Mama very calmly replied, "Mr. Chatmon, my son has his arm in a cast from elbow to finger-tips and he couldn't blow his fist if his life depended on it."

Carl wore glasses 'n people were still ugly about such things 'n were always makin' fun of folks who had to wear spectacles. Mr. Chatmon really skint his ignorance 'cause he called Carl a four-eyed liar. Mama moved up in the bus 'n without ever using a cuss word, she cussed him out so's his hide wouldn't'a held shucks.

33

I thought the old man was gonna tote Carl to school in his arms, he was so glad to get Mama shed of the bus. It seemed warmer all day long in the bus 'n old man Chatmon was nicer to us all 'n even changed the sand in the bottom of Ironsides. When we got off the bus Friday afternoon, it sounded like eleven savages hit the ground . . . whoopin', hollerin', and runnin'. We had a lot of chores for the weekend, but we would get in a heap of playing, too.

I headed for the feedhouse 'n got my chinaberry gun, so I could put the finishing touches to it. I had been careful to pick out a piece of cane that a chinaberry would fit snuggly into. I whittled the plunger 'n scraped it with a piece of glass 'til it was slick as a possum's hide. All I needed now was to fit it together 'n put a knob on the plunger. Well, before dark, I'd have it ready to fire.

Papa called out just as I finished. It was time to gather eggs 'n start the other duties. I slipped a berry bullet in the cane barrel 'n pulled the plunger back and pushed hard. The shoat jumped 'n grunted as the chinaberry hit his rump. Papa said he'd try it on me if he ever caught me using any more animals to better my aim!

I stuffed my homemade gun in my hip pocket 'n headed for the henhouse. Papa never lied to me 'n he had an uncanny way of explaining things where he didn't ever have to tell you but once. We ran out of chores 'bout the time Mama had supper ready. After we ate, we all went back to Papa's bedroom 'n listened to the radio. We could stay up 'til the "Gospel Singers" from WSM finished their hymns and we'd know it was our sign to go to bed. The deep-voiced man who said what they was gonna sing always sold snuff 'n a "cure-all" salve in between songs. The best cure for poison ivy I ever used was casin' head gas.

Morning came with all dogs barking, cows lowing, roosters crowing, 'n everything else joining the chorus, including Mr. Luther's mufflerless Chevy. But the best part was the smell of Mama's biscuits calling us outa bed.

Soon as I hit the floor, I knew it had come a killin' frost by the feel of my feet. Well, it'd make persimmons and collards sweeter to the mouth. I heard the voice of the old man from down in the Colony braggin' on how good Mama's cookin' was and he believed them wuz the best syrup he'd ever et. I never did know what his other name was 'cause we jus' called him Uncle Bud and he'd help Papa do things like fence mendin', killin' and scraping hogs 'n such. Us boys knew we'd have to make haste to the kitchen if we were to get our share, 'cause Uncle Bud never had a mind to quittin' when he passed his portions.

We all sat down, grabbing for everything in reach under Papa's scowl, but he let it pass 'cause he'd set a table more 'n once with his helper 'n it was only fair to side with kin.

After breakfast, I lit out, half doing my chores so's I could have a bigger part of play, and headed for Cack's with my new china gun 'n a pocketful of berries. There was nuthin' like a log barn to find good moving targets, 'specially in a corn crib. There was always rats stealing grain and you could knock 'em winding with a well-aimed china gun. I had been scoring about one outa three, which wadn't bad for a new weapon. Cack was using a sling 'n rocks, but he was gettin' three outa three and none of his targets ever got up. I heard Mama's voice floatin' cross the pasture, "Harry . . . Hareeee Boy, come home." When she got down to business on hailing you, it was best to give up 'n go to the house. 'Sides, I was down to my last berry. So I popped ole Cack with my last round 'n he helped me over the fence with his sling. He was a good buddy and was always givin' somebody a "lift" 'n his aim was as good as his friendship. I was still rubbing where he helped me when I got home.

✝   ✝   ✝

To delegate power does not guarantee delegation of wisdom.

Bound To You

I feel a sorrow for the wild thing as
it flies to a marsh or bay
flying farther from you, forever gone,
and I the lucky one choose to stay

because I am bound to you
not because I cannot fly
not because I walk the earth
nor countless other reasons why . . .

There is this that keeps me near,
this that keeps me true
I am bound—forever bound—
for I'm in love with you.

The old adage "You only live once" should be sufficient
advice to make you want to live right.

†　　　†　　　†

It's not how much money you spend on your wed-
ding . . . it's how much time you invest in your marriage that
makes it a long-term endowment.

†　　　†　　　†

The true test of love is to live with someone in affluency,
for in poverty, even those who abhor each other cling together for sheer existence.

†　　　†　　　†

If my sins are a stumbling block to my fellow man, it
didn't take much to trip him.

36

SHEPPARD'S STORE

Mama was standing on the veranda when I crawled through the barbed-wire fence. She had her hands on hips with an "I-work-my-fingers-to-the-bone-and-you're-never-here-to-eat-when-the-food's-hot" look on her face. But she let it pass 'n wanted to know why I was rubbin' my backside 'n if I had torn my overalls on the fence. Seemed like sometimes she was more interested in my breeches than my back. Course, hide would heal over. Soon's she got past her lecture, she told me she 'n Papa 'n Betty Gene were going to Sheppard's for flour. The way she leaned on it for baking, you'da thought she was a sold-out sinner with doomsday on her back. I commenced to begging 'n got to make the ride.

Papa switched on the key 'n pulled on the baling wire choke sticking out of the radiator 'n lifted up on the crank. It took three tries before the "T" kicked off. Papa flipped his leg over the side 'n before long he had both levers pulled down 'n was throwing rocks even on the straights. When we rounded Sicard Curve, the old car's wheels 'uz laying on their sides. As Mr. Luther'd say, "That scaffer was fair more flying." We musta been doing thirty miles an hour!

We pulled in to Sheppard's store 'n Papa cut the "T" off 'n sat 'til it quit running. Then he swung his leg over the side, which was our signal we could get out, too.

Mrs. Sheppard met us at the door. She was like kin to us. Mr. Huber was propped back in his cane-bottom chair by the hole in the floor. He chewed 'n could spit through that little old opening 'n never stain a board. I always did admire his aim.

Mr. Huber reached for the winding ball jar 'n gave me 'n Betty Gene one apiece. He was always givin' us candy when we came in, which'd make beggin' for the trip worth it. Papa paid some on his bill 'n let the rest ride. Mama'd always buy 'bout as much again, but this was a new charge 'n didn't count. I often wondered how many folks they'd fed during

37

the Depression. They was kinda' like the bank, 'cept they loaned groceries 'n didn't take no wagon or cows or nuthin' to back up a buy, 'n Lord knows, they ain't never took back a human being on a past-due food bill.

Mama finally finished talkin' 'n buyin' 'n we toted the stuff out to the old car and headed back to Swartz. When we passed Joe White's Road, I heard Papa tell Mama they'd be a baptizing Sunday afternoon right past the bend in Bayou DeSiard. Well, no matter what the signs said, there sure wouldn't be much fishin' going on near this part once they got started. The more folks they ducked under, the muddier the bayou got 'n it seemed it'd be hard for the preacher to tell if a body's sins were being washed away for the moss 'n stuff caught in their hair and overalls.

Mama had already had all us kids sprinkled 'n I never told nobody I never felt nuthin' 'cause nobody really told me much . . . only that I had been accepted by the congregation. But it'd be a long time 'fore I was accepted by the Lord. Course, it had its good points, being a member of a town church, 'cause we just got to go now 'n then and it was such fun being a heathen with an excuse.

Papa was a Baptist 'n sometimes I walked to church with him. It was on the Pelican Highway towards Wham Hill 'n had its cemetery right beside it so's if you had a funeral, you didn't hafta drive all over the country for the burying.

I liked Loch Arbor Church, 'specially when Mr. Jinks sang. He had such a deep voice the timbers would tremble. I liked to hear Papa sing, too. He was singing as he drove us back to the house and just knowing Mama had new flour had brightened us all.

When we got home, there was a big crowd in our front yard. All the young'uns were laughin', but the mamas were all shakin' their heads. Soon's we got out the car, we could see what had happened. The end of our garage was gone!

Mr. Oatly was the boss over at the plant 'n when he got to drinkin', he'd drive around 'til he found a garage with a back in it 'n just drive on through it. Nobody knew where he'd strike next.

One day, Charlie left his anvil right outside the back of his garage 'n Mr. Oatly like to never got it out of his radiator. Charlie swore he'd forgot about it, 'specially with the sharp end pointed jus' right. It broke Mr. Oatly's habit . . . not his drinking, just his drive-through desires.

† † †

Those who are fearless only in areas in which they have complete control have very little control in any situation in which they feel fear.

† † †

The basic needs of today are no different from the day man first discovered fire . . . only the flame of desire burns brighter.

† † †

Whichever we are—"stay-at-homes" or "cross-country commuters"—everything we catch or lose is caused by viruses or computers.

† † †

Each great leader of the past may have been superior only in his time. Those we consider mediocre today may have been the empire builders of yesteryear and those who were the kings of old could today be kindly old gentlemen next door with a taste for caviar.

† † †

If I had one worldly, material, commercial wish, it would be to design a toy that has the magic appeal of a cardboard box to a boy.

39

The Stately Strippers

The oak trees swayed and acted out
an exotic striptease show
to the music of a winter's wind
that moved them to and fro.

The prudish pines clung to their wraps
as the norther whistled its song.
Why! They wouldn't strip to a stranger's tune;
somehow it seemed so wrong.

But the oaks danced on and on
caught up in a frenzied pace.
The evergreen holly blushed with its berries
and seemed to turn its face.

Finally the striptease was over
and the oaks were standing bare.
They turned to face the prudish pines
with their haughty, self-righteous air.

They looked upon the naked oaks
and tried to bring them shame.
The oaks took an encore more
and smiled at their new-found fame.

For they knew that very soon
with the coming of the Spring,
a new green gown they'd wear
to wait for their winter's fling.

When they would dance and dip and strip
and shed their faded gown.
For they won't care what the others think
when the norther comes to town.

SIC 'EM GUINEA

We had three kinds of watchdogs when I was a boy—curs, hounds, and guinea hens. The guineas were the best. You couldn't slip up on 'em even if you were as quiet as a spider's spinning wheel. Besides, they could fly!

Once they heard a strange noise, they'd purr rack, purr rack, purr rack. It'd wake the dead and scare the living to death . . . 'specially at night.

I trained one to hunt squirrels and he turned out to be the best squirrel guinea I ever saw. He'd not only tree 'em, he'd fly up on the limb and show me where they were hiding. I finally trained him to point birds.

He had only one fault . . . he was the worst braggart I have ever heard. One day out at the barn, this loose-beaked bird got to boasting about how he had put the point on some local quail and was so engrossed in his prowess as a hunter that he failed to notice the stealthy approach of a jealous bird dog, which pounced upon the silly guinea and devoured him . . . thus ending the career of the best bird-bird I have ever known.

May happiness be your companion,
and the dregs in your drink lie deep.
May the one you love live at your house,
and may God watch over your sleep.

May the Lord bless your loved ones
and keep them forever in mind.
May He keep you always in love
and warm as the sun as it shines.

These are strange times! Everything keeps going up but nothing's going on.

† † †

A man should retire not because of his age in life but only his stage of life.

† † †

Old sayings like "Let the chips fall where they may" may have been the first littering of our country.

† † †

How man has survived his attempt to become extinct is a miracle when you think how successful he has been in destroying so many other species.

† † †

Those who buy less than they can afford, eat less than than they want, and spend less than they make are usually rich, slim smartasses!

† † †

Not many years ago, it was "more or less" taken for granted that one had to have character. Nowadays, the "moralless" are taken for granted.

† † †

Make each moment count, for many seconds pass that carry nothing more with them than the last breath of a man.

† † †

There are many steps that mark the progress of mankind . . . and most of them need sweeping around.

† † †

Read, converse, meditate. One should run a mental mile each day. More important than the physical, the mind can carry you to heights your legs will never climb.

If you're tired of reading, why don't you get up and try one of these????

Butter Biscuits

2/3 stick of butter
1 1/2 cups plain flour
1 1/2 tsp. baking powder
1/4 tsp. soda
1/4 tsp. salt
1 tsp. sugar
1 package dry yeast
2/3 cups buttermilk

Mix all dry ingredients and sift. Add two tablespoons very warm water to yeast, dissolve, and place in measuring cup. Add enough oil to make 1/3 cup. Finish filling cup with buttermilk. Stir in dry ingredients. Knead, roll, cut, and dip in melted butter, fold and bake at 450° until golden brown.

Nutmeg Honey Pancakes

1 1/2 cups plain flour
1 1/2 tsp. baking powder
1/2 tsp. salt
1/4 tsp. nutmeg
2 tbsp. honey
1/3 cup cooking oil
1 1/2 cups milk
2 eggs

Separate eggs, placing yolks in large mixing bowl. Add honey and mix thoroughly, adding milk and stirring briskly. Sift all dry ingredeints into liquid and add oil. Beat egg whites until they peak. Fold into batter and cook on a hot griddle.

43

Collards !!

Wait 'til after a good hard frost makes them sweet to the mouth. Break off each leaf without bruising the stalk.

Wash and drain, place in pot (black cast iron preferred), press down, and add ½ cup water, 1 teaspoon salt. Lace two or three slices of bacon across top of greens, then place a jalapeno pepper on top.

When greens are cooked to the chewy stage, lift them very tenderly and let drain. Now squeeze a lemon over the mound, then place a good generous cut of butter right smack on top.

My friend, this ain't soul . . . this is body food!

Now that you're full, it's time to relax and read some more.

You have reached middle age when you look down to see where the coffee spill spotted your shirt and find it missed your chest and was caught by your stomach.

† † †

Those who catch very few fish go fishing very few times.

† † †

Diamonds may be a girl's best friend, but gold has a weigh with everyone.

† † †

Stupidity is not distrubuted solely to those who serve. It is also shared among those who rule.

† † †

Boring your friends with the details of a recent operation has great therapeutic value, especially if you survived.

† † †

The hunger pangs of a man can be disguised with a smile, but the empty belly of a boy growls with a cry.

† † †

My son has an uncanny ability to sense cash in my money clip and forthwith clips me for my cash.

† † †

Money is called the root of all evil, but it's evil the way I have to root for my money.

† † †

Sometimes what we would possess the most is lost from us forever because of our possessiveness.

† † †

A snowball starts from the first snowflake that stuck and an avalanche from the last one that didn't.

NO RAIN CHECKS

Dawn came in crying as the wild things awoke and started stirring. Silhouettes were the only means of identification. Ducks with whistling wings were overhead, chattering to each other, and the flocks on the swamp were inviting them to breakfast. The feed call was like thousands of mini-machine guns rattling away. A lone figure of a man could be seen easing through the muddy waters, pulling a long cotton sack filled to heaviness.

He had lost count of how many ducks he'd killed . . . must be at least 150 or more. This was the third morning he had gotten up before day and caught the birds in their resting area and, come tomorrow morning, he'd be back if the moon held bright.

His head darted from side to side, ever watchful of the law. Seeing no one, he tugged at the heavy sack as he cleared the water and stepped on higher ground. He dropped the strap and reached for a cigarette, striking the match with his thumbnail. He cupped his hands around the flame, drawing deeply at the tobacco. His lungs rebelled and he bent in pain, trying to muffle the long racking cough that followed.

There were many eyes watching his every move. All but four were wild. A man was standing half hidden by a tree some fifty feet farther up the trail. His heavy shoulder was outlined under the thick jacket he wore. His hand, like a ham, hung at his side. He had found a parked car up in a thicket and knew the driver was up to no good. So he planted himself along the path and became a part of the swamp and waited. He had watched the poacher struggle with his burden for the past hour. Falling down, cursing softly, only to get up and slip and pull and fall again.

The figure took one more long drag, coughed, and flipped the butt into the murky water. He poked the toe of his boot through the strap and lifted it to his hand. With a sigh, he slung the strap over his shoulder and bowed his back to the

46

chore. Silently the warden waited. The poacher was half smiling as he labored with his load. Just a few hundred feet more and he would have the wild game loaded in his old car and be headed to Monroe.

The kill would bring a pretty good price from folks who liked to buy ducks and not ask questions. He was about a yard from the tree when the warden stepped out. A cruel contrast in health and handicap: on one side a picture of complete masculinity, on the other, a cripple of polio. The sight of the man caught the hunter completely by surprise, and before he could recover his composure, the good hand had shot out like a striking snake and locked on his wrist. The young man struggled . . . cursing, snatching, slinging the older man to the ground. But the grip never slackened. The warden couldn't keep his balance with his withered leg and, unable to ward off limbs with his crippled arm, he began to bleed from several cuts caused by the falls. There was one thing for sure . . . if Bo got hold of you, you belonged to him—because nothing would make him turn loose except your giving up. Finally, with a whimper of defeat, the younger man gave in, grunting, almost nauseous from the fight.

Bo twisted the young man's arm until he lay still upon the muddy ground and then sat down on top of him. Between deep gulps of air, the warden said, "Now, son . . . I want to see . . . your license." The poacher reached for his wallet and dug out a hunting permit, but no duck stamp. Bo daubed at the blood on his face. He dug into his jacket for his notepad and copied the name and address. He took his prisoner's shotgun and, pushing with it, straightened himself upon his good leg and motioned the culprit to move out.

With the ducks loaded into the Model A roadster, they started to town . . . a far cry from what the hunter had had in mind. All the hours of cold, wet wading through the black swamp, pulling that soggy sack of birds, every muscle aching, just to get a few lousy pennies from a bunch of no-good people who tried to buy them for less than the shells had cost. They were just as guilty, but they were warm and safe in bed.

The poacher threw his head back and laughed. Bo looked at him in wonder. The hunter said softly, "Sorry, Ma'am, no ducks today to entertain your high falutin' friends."

"What?" asked Bo.

"Nothing," replied the hunter, "Just catching my breath."

Bo grinned for he was happy he'd caught this hunter, but he wasn't the one he was after.

As the car sped along "Thunder Road," another hunter was moving toward higher ground from the depths of Boggy Bouef. He had watched with mixed emotions as the other man had fallen into the snare of the warden. He hadn't recognized the poacher and couldn't care less who he was . . . he got what he deserved, the stupid idiot. He had felt a flood of resentment as he thought, "A whole day ruined by this outsider."

Doug was a boy raised in the swamp. He was a free agent, wild as the woods he roamed, with an uncanny ability to read the signs of nature. A strong, graceful, broad-shouldered young giant, his bluejeans fit him as though they had been tailor-made.

He had killed more than 100 ducks. All mallards . . . mostly greenheads. He didn't kill just ducks, he killed mallards. And not on the water . . . he got his on the wing. His clientele was of much higher calibre than a common poacher's. Besides, these were his ducks, his swamp, his woods, and neither Bo nor anyone else could stop him, much less catch him. It wasn't just the game he killed, it was the game he played. He was the hunter for those who could not compete with nature. He was the Robin Hood of the rich and a friend to everybody. He could drink all night, yet wake up sober, bright-eyed and laughing.

Even old Bo liked him. Bo had been crippled back as long as folks could remember. He was devoted to God and his mother, dedicated to his patrol, catching friend and foe alike. His left arm hung useless by his side, sometimes getting in his

48

way. He hobbled in a grotesque way, but he asked no quarter and gave none . . . for, above all else, Bo was a man.

Doug slid the long cotton sack upon the trail, and when he stepped from the icy waters, one could see he was barefoot. He moved over to a log and felt beneath it with his feet, as a man will feel alongside his bed for his slippers. Finding them, he hooked his toe over the footgear and pulled them from their hiding place. He wiped his feet on the rough bark of the log and stepped softly into his Indian-fashioned moccasins, whistling like duck wings between his teeth. He began the task of hauling his kill to his auto.

Soon loaded, he started his roadster—almost a twin to Bo's—and backed from the underbrush where he had concealed it. Once out on the gravel highway, he switched the key on and off, causing the engine to backfire. "Boom, boom, boom" . . . thus the name "Thunder Road." It was Doug's way of calling to Bo, "I've done it again."

This morning he didn't really have any heart in his challenge to the warden, for he knew that by now, Bo was most likely seeing to the lodging of his duck shooter in the parish jail, arranging to give the game to the Children's Home.

Clouds moved into the area and the rain fell in torrents. The ducks got a breather from the night hunters and both Bo and Doug fretted away their time.

The third morning of rain arrived with the reinforcement of a new cold front that turned the downpour to sleet and snow. Bo was at the Red Store, drinking a cream soda, when the familiar "boom, boom" resounded outside. The next one through the door was Doug. He went straight to the "coke box," white teeth shining as he smiled, pulled out a cream soda, opened it, and joined Bo at the fire.

"Not much going on, huh, Bo?" Doug remarked. Bo cocked his head and grinned, "Naw, Doug, a man would be crazy to be out in this."

Everyone had noticed Doug's bluejeans were frozen up to

49

above his knees. Nobody said anything. "You had any ducks this year, Bo?" Doug asked.

"Naw, the season's not open yet," Bo replied.

"That's right. Well, when it opens and if I can remember, I'll kill you a mess, " the younger man promised.

Everyone looked at Bo, but he just took another drag of his cream soda and said, "That's real good of you, Doug. Thanks."

Doug finished his drink and placed the bottle in the rack. "I guess I'll go take a nap. Didn't sleep much last night."

The door opened to the south, but the cold wind was whipping at the light snow as the younger man started to leave.

Bo called after him, "Drive carefully in this. It's mighty bad out there."

Doug turned, grinned, and said, "Yeah, Bo, this is fowl weather."

Nobody said anything for a while . . . just stood around the fire and thought about this young man who didn't believe what he did was wrong. The crop of ducks had arrived and this was harvest time. Then there was the older man, crippled only in his body, with a fierce dedication to his duty of enforcing the law. They wondered who would win.

The morning woke up raining and Bo was drinking coffee. He knew this would be a day for Doug. Hobbling out to his car, he crawled up in the seat and shivered beneath his slicker and cold weather gear. He marveled at Doug's stamina, knowing that at this moment he was probably wading barefoot in the swamp, methodically harvesting the hunted. Shifting into reverse, he felt the dull sound that could only be a flat tire. Doug would get a head start on him this morning if he didn't hurry.

Bo tumbled out of his car, reaching for the screw type jack and lug wrench. When he started to loosen the bolts he noticed a long black locust thorn imbedded in the casing. He would have to be more careful where he drove. He hurriedly

50

changed to the spare, threw the tools back inside the "A," and ground the gears, trying to make up for lost time.

The sky was completely overcast as he wrestled the old Ford around the corner on Stubbs-Vinson Road. "Boom, boom, boom." Bo heard the backfiring on Thunder Road. Doug had gotten the jump on him. He jammed the accelerator to the floor. He would give him a chase anyway. When Bo hit the crossing at Peerless Plant, the "A" bounced like a ball, almost causing him to lose control. The rain was coming down in a steady pour and visibility was zero.

Bo topped the hill on Thunder Road and, just as he got into the curve, he saw Doug's Model A on its top across the ditch. He tromped the brakes and skidded dangerously close to the road's edge. Throwing the gears in reverse, he backed up even with the wreck and tumbled out, hobbling across the rain-filled drainage ditch. Bo was mumbling . . . "Oh God, Doug, Oh God." When he got to the boy, he could see Doug's neck was broken. Jerking off his slicker, he covered the body as best he could and then noticed a sack of ducks hanging out of the rumble seat. Bo quickly pulled the heavy sack of birds out and, half falling, half tumbling, dragged them over to his own car and dumped the ducks into it. If he couldn't catch Doug while he was alive, there was damn well nobody gonna catch him now.

Folding the sack into a square, Bo hobbled back to Doug and placed it under his head. Rain was pelting down so hard one could scarcely see the tears on the old warden's face. As he pulled himself erect, the thunder rolled, "Boom, Boom, Boom."

Bo looked back at the hunter and said softly, "Goodbye, Doug. I'll take your ducks to the Children's Home."

The sun shone brightly on the day of the funeral. The pallbearers placed their boutonnieres on the casket and a hush fell over the crowd as Bo struggled forward to place a green feather on top of the rest, then turned and wobbled away.

51

Duck season was about over and Bo just didn't seem the same. Oh, he went through the motions of being a game warden, but the old challenge was gone for him and he seemed to be listening for the backfire on Thunder Road.

He went by the Red Store, had a cream soda, and talked to the boys.

"Looks like rain again, Bo," Uncle Tip predicted. "Yep, just might do that, Uncle Tip," Bo half-heartedly replied.

"Boom, boom, boom, " the thunder rolled.

Bo looked startled and, without a word, limped to his old car.

Later that evening, his brother came by looking for him. The rain was fierce and one could hardly see now. "If you see him, Wilson, tell him I'm looking for him." Then as an afterthought, he added, "I think I'll swing down Thunder Road for a check."

Fred had been worrying about Bo lately.

It was then he saw the tracks where a car had skidded off the gravel road. Bo was lying on his back, a peaceful look on his face. Water was running off the wrecked automobile, down the fresh ruts it had plowed 'til it met the ones Doug's car had made, and running together until it mixed with the stream-swollen ditches.

Fred reached out to touch him and noticed a green feather clutched in his brother's hand.

The game had been called on Thunder Road . . . rained out.

"Boom, boom, boom," the thunder rolled.

†   †   †

So smoothe the glib tongues of our enemies. So like the silken yarn from the spider's spinning wheel . . . and as deadly in design.

The Warmth of Love

In the winter's unconcern
trees are standing in their bare.
Wild things hurry, stirring
as they scurry here and there.

In the morning's earth turn
wild geese flying in the high sky
small birds winging, singing,
and a blue teal whirring by . . .

So the setting is befitting
for a warm and tender time
as I hold you in the mental
in the cold, indifferent clime.

As my thoughts embrace and love you
I see a strange thing that it brings.
The lifeless twigs start budding
as tho' suddenly it's Spring.

The more mature my children become, the fewer my
virtues seem to be . . . until only my generosity is left uncri-
ticized.

† † †

Each of us has a ticket on a train called Destiny. Some
won't ride very far, others will ride for a longer time, and
some will seem to ride forever. Yet each of us has only two
choices at debarkation time—and one is a hell of a place to
get off.

PREACHIN' & PRAYIN'

My shoulders ached from the severe cold. I pulled at the heavy quilts to cover my exposed parts and saw icicles hanging from the homemade awnings I had fashioned from pieces of tarpaulin. This was the first winter I was to spend in the room I had built at the end of the porch. I had a canvas wall between me and Mother Nature and she was a cold one to sleep with. There comes a time, though, when a boy has to move out of the room with his brothers and I had picked this season!

I shivered at the thought of getting out of bed. My shoulders still hurt deep and numb and I could well imagine how cold the floor was going to be. Well, it was now or in just a minute, so I hit the floor seconds before Papa's call.

I grabbed my jumper and overalls and headed for the fire. Next time, I'd hang my clothes inside. At least they'd be warm when I got in 'em. Seemed like Mama always had coffee brewed and two big swigs began to thaw me out. I got me a biscuit and a sausage and wadded myself up by the fire again. There was no way to get enough warmth to last through a milking and I had that coming, 'cause I could hear the calves' mama calling me.

I hated cold weather . . . I believe I'da died in my cradle if I'd been an Eskimo. Well, anyhow, this was Friday and if the snow held, we'd be rabbit hunting tomorrow.

When I got to the feedhouse, I could hear my brother Carl bitching about how cold his hands was, and the cows didn't like it either. Well, if misery loves company, it was gonna get some 'cause I'd just arrived with a new batch. I rinsed the cow's teats off with my bucket of warm water, dried 'er off, and squatted down at her flank with the milkpail between my legs, being careful to tuck her tail in my bent knees. I never did like to be hit with a frozen cow's tail full of cockleburrs. She immediately began working to get it loose.

Our old tomcat inched closer and closer. I started a stream of milk toward him. He'd lick at the air 'til he got the right beam and follow the flow up to where I could, with one good squirt, give him a milk bath. Then he'd run get on the gatepost and bathe himself with those great soft paws of his. He allus did trust me, though, and I'd get him again this evening.

I was awakened from my catnap by a cockleburr club across my ear. After the first shock left me, I drew back and hit Old Brindle in the belly that made her reach for her cud. She just rapped me again and I gave up and put her tail in jail again 'n finished milking.

I hurried to the house, taking care not to slosh the milk out, 'cause the cream was on top. Some of the young'uns who didn't hafta milk were already waiting for the old bus, their breaths sending out little clouds of conversation.

Someday I was gonna own me a house in town and I wasn't never gonna milk no more and I was gonna take me a bath every morning and every night and the whole thing was gonna be inside the house and milk delivered at the door, too.

Saturday was just as cold, but it didn't seem like it 'cause we were gonna track rabbits in the snow. I called old Strib and Ham Dog up. They knew it was a good day to hunt, too. We didn't have to go far before the dogs gave chase and about a half-hour later, we found 'em scratching around the hollow of an oak tree. I dug in my jeans for my Barlow knife and cut me a sapling about finger size and ten feet long, and trimmed all the limbs off 'cept the two I bobbed off for a fork. I fed it up the hollow 'til it touched something soft and started twisting. I got a good hold of fur and kept winding and pulling and fighting off dogs until I drug the rabbit out of his hiding place. I allus wondered why God made rabbits with such pitiful looking eyes. I'da turned the pore thing loose if it hadn't been for my mouth, but I could already taste that rascal fried and gravy and all. We caught three more and lit out for the house. We skinned 'em, making sure we didn't hair the meat, and took 'em to Mama.

Papa'd put some heart in saying the blessing tonight . I marveled at the way he'd say thanks over leftover tripe. I allus hated tripe . . . it was tough anyway you pulled at it. I never believed the Maker expected a man to say Grace over a fresh mess of tripe, much less leavings. Oh, well, tonight we'd have hominy 'n greens 'n things.

Tomorrow we was gonna go to church to hear this big Texan preach. He wore a big white hat 'n talked about deer 'n dogs 'n he could hit the altar so hard it'd scare hell out of you. Most everybody slipped their hands up when he asked if anybody needed praying for. The way he'd talk about Catholics, I swear I thought they were worse than the devil; but my friend Newty was one, and when he told me how they were 'n they were most like us 'n headed in the same direction, I really started worrying about 'em and wished they could go hear this big feller holler. 'Sides, we knew they'd call on Mr. Wes to pray and we'd count how many times he cleared his throat while he was doing it.

Many a time, I bet, God turned to his Son and said, "I got fifty-two this time . . . how many'd you git?" 'n Mama called us to supper.

All Before the Green

Oh, chill so deep and not from cold . . .
This winter's wind is from the old
and time is such a tease and fast.
How quickly summer rushes past.
Now it's autumn and leaves of gold
so beautiful, so fragile, their story told,
some leaves cling on almost till spring
But they all turn loose before the green . . .
all before the green.

So it is with you and I.
We're born to live, grow old, and die.
But some of us will never sing
or know the joys that peace can bring.
For wars or killing kind will prey
upon the race of man and slay
many young ones in their teens.
But we all turn loose before the green . . .
all before the green.

There will be others who live to tell
of many autumns and friends who fell
in the cycle, birth till death,
some in poverty, some in wealth.
Few will ere be famous, most without
        acclaim,
and in the final hours all will be the
        same.
Whatever we are or might have been,
we all turn loose before the green . . .
all before the green.

BULLY WAS MY BROTHER

Tony's old open truck loaded with greens 'n fruit 'n stuff was almost devoured by the dust from the dirt road as he chugged off to sell somebody else "somating a fixa for eat."

He had given me the prize of this trip . . . an old banana stalk almost black from age. The henhouse was full of mites and that was as good a way to ward 'em off as an asafetida bag for any condition or a "buck-eye" for good luck.

Durn Dominique hens raised the devil at me when I entered their house. They could make as much fuss as a guinea hen. They'd bitch about anything, but a guinea was lots better as a watchdog. Well, they'd be rid of the mites in a week. 'Sides, Mama had said no more cakes or pies 'til they's run off. She always could bargain dirty.

I eased past the roost so as not to pick up any bugs and hung the stalk and walked on out by the feedhouse. Bully was chewing his cud. I pulled his tail and took off. He'd always chase me. I'd run between the milkshed 'n barn 'n fence. Bully couldn't sidle through, so I'd run on around, sneak up behind him, yank his tail again and run like a "yonder-it-goes." He'd hightail right after me and get stuck again. Soon he caught on and, instead of following me, he'd hide in the milkshed and as I'd make the circle, he'd rush out and butt me. I got to where I thought of old Bully as a brother.

I never will forget. One night after Papa had called on God to bless our supper, I looked up and there was grits 'n gravy and the biggest platter of meat seen in a coon's age.

Lordy, I dug in. Finally, I asked Mama where we got this much steak. Papa said, "Shut up and eat. I killed old Bully today."

"You killed old Bully! " I cried. And with tears running down my cheeks, I got me another helping.

A Depression, I thought, would make you kill your kin.

A love that lasts must be cared for. It's a sharing thing . .
a final sip of wine or a broken piece of bread. Only two, me
and you. You must give all but not take all in return, for to
give all is love . . . to receive, a loving.

† † †

Because we love someone, we do things for them
whether or not they love us. It's just more fun if they do.

† † †

If you put too much "I" in anything you're trying to
run, you'll most likely ruIn it.

† † †

Each day I live I find I am closer to the philosophy that
every good has something better and every bad has something
worse and I try to stay somewhere in between.

† † †

Each tyrant of the past came into power because of an
apathetic people or a superior weaponry. I believe if Hitler
had been born in prehistoric times, he would have been just
another sissy with a spear.

† † †

One should not curse the catch of those who keep their
bait wet.

† † †

When our young reach college, we cannot teach. We
must create desire and then they will learn.

† † †

I cannot accept suicide. Why buy a ticket for some place
when you have a free trip there anyway?

† † †

If you have to ask a lady whether or not her beauty
treatments are working, you both know they aren't.

NOT GUILTY

The night was as dark as a tomb, except for the occasional flash of lightning and the constant pink glow of the carbon plant "hot houses" against the low, angry clouds boiling overhead. Several times a zig-zag bolt had split the air and run up and down the tin backbone of the warehouses, followed by the rumble of thunder. Then another silver saber would slice the darkness and grumble through the metal sheds.

Three white men, their faces blackened by carbon, peered into the darkness with zombie eyes made even more ghostly by the white powder they had dusted themselves with to keep the carbon from becoming embedded in their pores. Their anxiety grew as they watched His wrath lash out. One man was visibly shaken each time the lightning struck. The reason lay not twenty-five feet from where he stood. A tub had been turned upside down over a goose and it loomed like a mountain in the eerie light. Two weeks had passed since the bird had wandered innocently into the plant yard and had been promptly impounded under the tub.

The crew had been waiting with much anticipation for a taste of this roasted delicacy! Spike Mitchie was the jailer and he had been gathering any and all leftovers from the lunch buckets to stuff the ill-fated fowl.

Tuh-loom-a-loom-a-loom, the thunder rolled on and on. Spike knew the hand of God was searching for his soul in this storm. Unable to endure the guilt that raged inside himself, he ran madly toward the tub—soaked before he reached the goose's metal jail—and flung the thing across the plant yard. The freed web-footed creature rose to its grandest ganderism and slowly walked away.

Spike dashed back to the safety of the press shed with the mascara of the carbon black running down his entire body. From out of the night, the fading voice of the goose

60

could be heard saying, "I thank you, I thank you, I thank you."

The moon broke through the clouds and Spike heaved a sigh of relief.

He had been acquitted.

I'll give you sunshine
        when it rains
I'll give you warmth
        when you are cold
I'll give you comfort
        when you are sad
I'll stay by your side
        when you grow old
I'll give you a breeze
        when the leaves grow still
I'll write you poems
        and songs and rhyme
I'll give you a smile
        if you should cry
And I'll give you love
        for all time.

On the fifth day
of July, 1972

My family tree has borne very few trouble-makers. Of course, I had an uncle thrown out of Town Hall a couple of times, but he was an uncle twice removed.

If we treated those we love while we are near them as though we would never see them again, we wouldn't waste another moment bickering.

† † †

Some people will say anything in order to be heard . . . even if it comes out like the bray of a jackass.

† † †

If you're not happy with your occupation, it's not necessary to change jobs . . . just attitude.

† † †

Praying when you're in trouble is like kissing your wife after you've laughed at her new coiffure. You're hanging a prayer on a hair.

† † †

Students should never try to overshadow their masters, for the moon is always at its darkest when it eclipses the sun.

† † †

I think all bad news should be banned until after noon. It's tough enough just getting up in the morning.

† † †

My customers may not all be right, but they're alright with me.

† † †

The fire of man is seldom kindled by dampened spirits— so drink it straight.

† † †

Major problems are seldom solved if minor differences are given precedence.

EMMALINE & NOBE

Several of us boys had been down to the creek chunkin' at turtles on logs 'n stumps. The sun was almost overhead and Mama had threatened us with a second cousin to a skinnin' if we didn't get home by dinner time. I cut 'cross the hill to shorten the odds 'n just as I hit the main road, I heard the familiar "ding-a-ling, ding-a-ling-ling."

Like a bee headed for the hive, I quickened my pace. I could get to the house and mooch Mama out of a nickel 'n still beat the bell ringer to the bridge. That is, if Mama didn't get stingy.

I made the mooch 'n before the door could slam was through the gate 'n strung out toward the Pelican Highway.

I caught up with the two down by Springhill Cemetery 'n hailed 'em. They stopped when they heard my call. "Uncle Nobe" was a chocolate-colored old gentleman 'n he walked everywhere with his croakersack full of small nickel-sized bags of peanuts. There was a young man who walked with him and carried another croakersack of extra supplies. 'Sides Nobe was blind.

"Hey, Uncle Nobe, hold up a minute, will ya?"

"Hi, boy, wanta sack?"

"Yessiree," I replied and asked, "are they good?"

"Are they good? Bes' in town, got 'em all toasted, nice 'n brown."

I walked slowly back to the house, eating as fast as I could. I didn't mind sharing, but if you didn't have nothin' left, you didn't have to go through the agony of parting with peanuts.

I could hear Uncle Nobe calling out, "Red hot 'n still a-heating, buy a sack 'n walk off eatin'." He never made a mistake in making change. Course, there wasn't many times he had to worry about dollar bills.

Mama was waiting for me on the veranda and said, "Boy, if you spoil your dinner with those peanuts, I'm going to skin you alive."

So, after Papa did the blessin', I worked on Mama's mission 'til she was satisfied I was full. When I was able to get excused from the table, I retrieved the four peanuts I had left in my cheek for dessert 'n walked out to the washpots.

Emmaline was boiling our overalls, pokin' 'em with a blue broomstick. She was singing an old spiritual, interrupting her singing only occasionally by switching her black gum twig. Emmaline dipped snuff 'n her twig kept it stirred. She was shiny black and her hair was tight, tiny curls that clung close to her head. She lived in a small cottage out from the company houses 'n I never knew her to have any special job. She just helped everyone in the quarters. She kept all the kids when folks had to go somewhere like funerals and things. I loved old Emma. She was always happy 'n had time to talk and listen. She'd play all kinds of games with us and you could hear her laughin' above all the other noises.

I was sitting on the old tub bench, swinging my legs back and forth and watching her work.

"Ya ever have any children?" I asked.

"Jus' y'all, honey. Y'all my chilren, evah one."

"Emmaline, how come you're black?"

" 'Cause God made me a nigger, Chile," she laughed.

"Are all niggers black, Emma?"

"Naw, Chile, we all colors. We got white blood, Indian blood, Catholic blood, Baptist blood . . . 'cept me, I'se puoredee black. But God loves me 'n His dye don't run 'cause I'se always gwine be black."

"I don't care, Emmaline. I don't care what color you are. I love you."

"I loves you, too, Chile. Lawd God knows, I loves you, too. Now fotch me one dose tubs so's I can dip out 'dese close."

I handed Emma a tub 'n walked off wondering what was God's favorite color. Musta' been blue, 'cause there was more sky 'n sea than any other color. Emmaline went back to her singing.

64

The Elusive Lure

I looked for love
in poems and song
with friends I met
as I wandered along.

Under stars at night
or the sunlit sky
in the valleys low
and the mountains high.

I looked for love
the elusive lure
that brings us fame
or leaves us poor.

I looked and called
and searched in vain
for a thing called love
in a world of pain.

I sipped at wine
and it didn't reveal
this thing called love
or the way I feel.

Then it came one day
as a gentle shove
for I kissed your lips
and I tasted love.

The older a man becomes, the more like a mule he seems—for he finds his services are limited to fewer people.

The most dangerous competitor is the one who has reached the point of not caring for personal gain or safety of position.

† † †

I would rather be dumbfounded than found dumb, because if you're the latter you will never overcome being the former.

† † †

The best advice I have ever received was that which coincided with my line of thinking.

† † †

I measure nothing by what it costs, only by what it's worth.

† † †

The worst failure in the world is the one who becomes a carbon copy of an unsuccessful superior for the sake of employ.

† † †

My daughter and her husband are determined to live within their budget even if they have to eat at my house.

† † †

I get along well with my friends by not lending anything I wouldn't borrow.

† † †

Many people are determined to make it on their own, but some are professional parasites . . . the former trying to climb the ladder of success and the others just content with the latter.

† † †

A new year is not unlike a blind date . . . mysterious, exciting, and usually a relief when it's over.

CRUMBS ARE CAKE, TOO

When the gasoline plant was built at Swartz, there were eight houses constructed to accomodate the day and night crews. Only two gangs were needed because each bunch worked twelve hours. Whoever chose the location of the quarters was not learned in urban improvement. A road was planned in front of the houses, but no one ever got around to building it. Also, the row of dwellings was situated to the northeast of the plant and the prevailing winds carried any and everything that would float, including noise. So, through the years, anyone who came home or came to see us entered the back door. The view one got out front was one of cowsheds, hog pens, gardens, and then the tree line. I still have trouble entering a front door of anything unless I'm carrying a pail of milk or fresh-gathered eggs or vegetables.

Between the plant and the quarters, there was an artesian well close to the fork of the road and it was the best water I can remember. The Morrows lived up the right fork across the creek from us, and we referred to them as Mama and Daddy Morrow. Mr. Morrow was a short, tank-like man with a corncob pipe that was strong enough to keep moths out of the house. Legend had it that he could cuss so good it would peel paint off a house. But not anymore! Now, when he got to a point of profanity, he would just "Dear-Dear." I have never seen such complete control.

Daddy Morrow was a well rider for the company and he would make the rounds every day—checking the charts at the meter houses, making sure each well was producing, and changing the charts. Then, on to the next one. If a road became impassable, he would simply cut across the woods and waller himself another one.

One evening, Mama had cooked a chocolate cake and since I was going to ride the wells with Daddy Morrow the next morning, she gave us half the three-layer to take along. He had just gotten a new canvas top Model A Ford pick-up truck. Hadn't even had it in the mud yet! We took off across country, from gravel roads to dirt ones, pig trails 'n log roads to nothin'. We came upon a bog that looked like it could swaller a sugar mule. Without slowing down, Daddy Morrow swerved to the right, through the brush. Now, he was a sight to behold! Old slouch hat, khaki riding pants stuck down in laced up leather boots that came up to his knees, corncob pipe billowing foul smoke, driving with one hand on the wheel and the other hanging on to the new canvas top, and me hanging on to anything in reach.

No sooner had he started through the woods, making himself a new road, than a low-hanging limb literally snatched the top from the pick-up. Grabbed it right out of his hand. Without even a howdy-do, he just "Dear-Dear" and kept slinging mud like a runnin' scared politician, bouncing up and down over logs 'n stumps. By 'n by we got back to a hard road. We stopped later on in the day in Perryville 'n got us a Nehi soda apiece and started looking for the cake. It wasn't anywhere in the pick-up. Then we decided to take out the seat cushion 'n there was a ball of something wadded up in the tool box. Mama's beautiful work of art had been kneaded into a mess rolled up in wax paper. I lifted it up and gently unrolled it across the hood of the baptized Model A. If we hadn't known it was a cake, we'da never recognized it. It looked like a dog's breakfast. We scratched it up in little piles of chocolate-covered crumbs and washed it down with Nehis. Mama's cake tasted just like it always did, but this time it was pre-chewed.

✝   ✝   ✝

I took a memory course once, but I can't remember why . . .

✝   ✝   ✝

To learn the art of being patient takes a lot of perserverance.

68

Man is indeed a strange creature. He tries to clean his soul on Sunday morning before he has cleared his Saturday night head.

† † †

There are no innocent bystanders in an angry mob of dissenters.

† † †

The tongue has been unwittingly accused many times for blurting an obscenity when, in truth, it was merely expelling something a foul mind had emptied upon it.

† † †

When my life on earth is over and I stand before the Heavenly Throne, I think I shall be fairly hacked if I discover that some of the so-called "sins" I have abstained from would not have given me a failing grade.

† † †

If I culled all my friends because of their faults, I wouldn't have a friend left. But that would be my fault.

† † †

Men wail and beg for mercy under the whip of a tyrant, yet they will take advantage of a good taskmaster until he is replaced by a hostile overseer.

† † †

If you want to know what makes a man tick, you've got to listen to the way he tocks.

† † †

God made man in many colors, but the thing we're all supposed to think with is called "grey matter." Seems to me, we ought to find some kind of answer there.

† † †

The best way to be subtle with your children is not to appear a'parent.

PLAY IT SOFTLY, PLEASE

Ned Masterson had been down to the Kinnerlys' house and he was telling his mother how good Mrs. Kinnerly could play a piano. He said, "But, Mama, she's so deaf, you have to holler at 'er to make 'er hear you."

Mrs. Masterson was a kindly woman, who was good to everyone, and she did love piano music as well as a body could. She told Ned she'd be obliged to go down there next afternoon if it would pleasure Mrs. Kinnerly.

Next morning, Ned stopped by to convey the message his mama had sent and added: "Please talk and play loud 'cause Mama's almost stone deaf."

Later on in the day, Mrs. Masterson showed up and Mrs. Kinnerly hollered her in. Well, sir, you could hear 'em screaming at each other for near a mile and the piano sounded like somethin' beset by the devil.

Next day Mrs. Masterson said with a hoarse voice, "Ned, Mrs. Kinnerly plays well, but she bangs away at the poor piano as though she were ravin' mad. And holler! My stars and garters, I've never heard a woman screech so. It'll be a cold day in May before I set foot there again."

Down the road, Mrs. Kinnerly was gargling with antiseptic for her strained throat and tryin' to explain to her husband why.

It would be six weeks before either one of 'em learned the other wasn't hard of hearing.

Ned would swear he never meant any harm, but when his mama finished flogging him, he knew she had!

The summer days dragged on like a three-legged terrapin. We canned peas 'n beans 'n things and put mayhaw 'n huckleberry jelly 'n jam in anything we could scald out and wax over.

The hogs were getting fat for their fall killing. Mama would can some sausage in oil and Papa would have us gather green hickory for smoking the rest.

The mash was plentiful, which was a good indication of a hard, cold winter. The okra in the garden had been pruned so high you had to bend the stalk to get a mess. Fall was close, if you were mindful of the signs.

Each time the breeze combed the trees, they became more bald, and soon the skies would have clouds of ducks and geese flying farther from the Northern Lights.

It wouldn't be long, on a cold clear winter's night, when we would hear Mrs. Kinnerly playing her piano again. But more softly now. . .

✝   ✝   ✝

The trouble with most critics is they think to criticize means only to condemn.

✝   ✝   ✝

My friends never disturb me except when they don't disturb me.

✝   ✝   ✝

If we can't control the situation, we should never let the situation control us.

✝   ✝   ✝

Oh, how clever are we behind our masks as we go about our obligatory tasks.

✝   ✝   ✝

Southerners have been called racists for such a long time it's accepted as a truth. I suppose to a degree it is, for I know a lot of blacks that don't like any white people.

✝   ✝   ✝

A "company man" may not always be the right man for the company.

71

I would condemn a man sooner for lack of compassion than lack of competence.

✝   ✝   ✝

Time heals all pangs of the poor if it puts a few coins in their pockets.

✝   ✝   ✝

Men make a big to-do about women's rights, but I wonder where men got that right, and more, what makes men think they're so right?

✝   ✝   ✝

If we can applaud our opponent in his hour of glory, we will be more noble in defeat than most are in victory.

✝   ✝   ✝

Man in his quest for progress has built the most convenient baths in the world and has fouled his water supply in the process.

✝   ✝   ✝

If you are in love with two women and one has beautiful eyes and the other a gorgeous figure and you are in doubt as to which one you should choose—remember, eyes don't get fat.

✝   ✝   ✝

When you wear your heart on your sleeve, you're bound to be cuffed on occasion.

✝   ✝   ✝

Fuel costs have increased so much, it's a toss-up as to which is worse . . . sweating out a summer or sweating out the bill.

✝   ✝   ✝

If a man is so complex, how come he's so simple-minded?

72

ROLLIN' GROCERY

A dipping vat for cattle was an awesome place made from cement, sand, rock, steel wire, and rods. Each was about 2½ feet wide and 20 feet long with a sharp drop off on the chute end and steps leading up to the exit. The most devastating feature of a vat was its contents. It was filled with a foul-smelling creosote mixture that would make eyes smart and noses sting, just smelling it.

The nearest vat to our place was about a quarter of a mile away. We'd drive the cattle down to the cut-off and head them up a lane. At its end was the corral that held the stock and then a chute which would guide them to their destined dipping.

We had everything we owned penned. Cows, bulls, calves, goats—all milling around 'bellerin', hookin' each other, wild-eyed and uneasy.

Each of us had a sturdy rod of hickory for prodding 'em on, keeping them on the move. Once you got them headed up the lane, it wasn't any trouble getting them in the dipping pen. They didn't have any other place to go except backwards and our sticks discouraged that.

Now, nobody nor nuthin' else alive that I've ever known ever developed a liking to havin' creosote in his eyes, much less jumping into a batch of it over his head. It never was easy to convince an old mama cow that it was what she needed. She didn't even know what tick fever was, much less care that this was a good preventive. Nevertheless, everyone of the animals had to get a chance to swim and we helped 'em make up their minds. The Counter was hanging over the chute where the cattle hurried out and it was his duty to see that every head of stock had a daub of green paint on their rumps then the range rider would know they had been obliged.

One thing for sure, dippin' wasn't the cure for everything. We had been feeding all the milk to the hogs and chickens, because the cows had been eating bitter weeds and the milk was like quinine. On days like this, Mama had to put sugar or molasses in her biscuits to keep them sweet.

Mama was always slicing salt meat and soaking it in sugared water so it'd be rid of most the salt and was sweet to the mouth come mornin'. I like the days when she would slice the leftover baked sweet potatoes and fry 'em in the deep fat from the bacon. That 'n salt meat 'n eggs was something to start a daybreak.

During the hot summer evenings, we usually had homemade ice cream, but the soured milk had played the devil with that for the past two weeks. Well, maybe by next Saturday we could have sweet milk again. We had changed the cows' pasturing up to the cedars and the grass was high'n sweet 'n tender up there.

Our old hand-cranked ice cream freezer was as noisy as a spooked cur-dog. On a still day, you could hear it for near a mile. You couldn't get more company if you mailed out invitations. We'd just get out more bowls 'cause we had waited as long as need be.

Papa woke me out of my daydream and told me to "watch what my end of the chores were." I got the old bell cow out first and the rest fell in behind, headed home.

When we got through separating the calves from their elders, we went in to wash up. The table was set and Mama had cooked hot water cornbread, with her finger marks in 'em, a pot of tender greens, crowder peas, chow-chow, sliced tomatoes 'n onions, and a gallon bucket of tea. Papa never left a word out of the blessing and I know he was as hungry as us!

We were about to finish eating when it sounded like all hell broke loose. A yearling that belonged to the Kinnerlys had run out in front of a "Rolling Grocery Store." The driver had slammed on the brakes and had thrown half his inventory up front where he was sitting.

Pickle juice was running out the front and down over the worn threshold where a trough had been worn by the many feet of yesteryear's children getting on and off the old school bus. Flour, meal, and snuff were over everything. The proprietor of the old converted bus sat sneezing, white-headed as a ghost from the dusting of a broken sack of self-rising.

If a body had wanted to get in the grocery business, this was as 'bout as good a time as ever. We finally got him outside and took a broom to him and his store. Broken glass, bent cans, busted sacks—he had a little of it all. The whole disaster wasn't as bad as first sight, though. And his business was soon off the "for sale" market and we were richer by a Baby Ruth candy bar apiece and the driver was on his way with a special sale on bent buckets.

Kinnerly's yearling never did know he'd served us candy for our dessert on dipping day.

† † †

One of the cruelest thefts perpetuated upon the United States citizen is the Social Security program. You don't get enough to be social and, by golly, you sure don't get enough to feel secure.

† † †

Nowadays people search through many coins looking for a rare dime. During my childhood, anytime I found one in my pockets, it was rare.

† † †

A fool and his fuel are soon parted.

75

Old age comes slow to some, quietly to others, fast to many, and almost never to those who are unmindful of it.

✝   ✝   ✝

He who tips his brew too often proclaiming "Bottoms Up" usually is showing same.

✝   ✝   ✝

Common sense sees the problem and solves it. Book sense surveys the same situation and orders new parts.

✝   ✝   ✝

To live without love is to die without hope.

✝   ✝   ✝

"If the shoe fits, wear it" may not be such a great idea if you're getting in over your head.

✝   ✝   ✝

The extension of one's self beyond self is more than life—it's living.

✝   ✝   ✝

If you're ashamed of where you're from, you ought to be ashamed of where you're going.

✝   ✝   ✝

In this push-botton age, the one we push the most is marked Panic.

✝   ✝   ✝

The backlash of Women's Lib will destroy our species when men demand equal rights to bear children.

✝   ✝   ✝

When people yell at me, I yell back . . . simply because I assume they are most certainly deaf and not vulgar.

LOOK OUT FOR LUTHER!

Mr. Luther was a self-made strong man. He didn't set out to be one. He just figgered there wasn't nothin' he couldn't pick up, so nature molded his body into a mountain.

He drove every car he owned as if Satan himself was pitch-forking him in the tail. One thing about him though was his constant safety factor. If Mr. Luther got his car right off the assembly line he would lose the muffler by the time he got to the curb. At least you could hear him coming.

When he cranked his car, he'd rev it up and the open exhaust pipe caused dust to boil all over his vehicle. Then out he'd pop and you never knew in which direction he'd be coming. So it'd be best to climb a tree or give him the road.

The road gang for the state had been working on the crossing at Long Bridge Creek which was about 35 feet across. Well, sir, Mr. Luther could be heard a-comin' one day—that ever increasing roar had to be his car. Sounded like a tornado approaching and looked like it, too, with all that dust boiling. There was a loud crash—then nothin' but silence. We broke and run to Long Bridge Creek, where we found him sitting in his car in the creek with a grin on his face. "Ya hurt, Mr. Luther?"

"Naw, I just forgot they took the bridge out! Like to 'a made it, though. I had that scaffer going like Dan after the Doctor."

The frame was bent in the middle, so that it always made the front of his car look like it was going uphill, while the back was going downhill. But it sure helped his dust boiler—'cause his exhaust was closer to the ground.

I always have wondered what a scaffer was!

† † †

To make a short story long—just keep talking.

77

To depart this world cost more than it does to arrive. Besides the extra expense, you can't get out of it alive.

† † †

The reason I don't like "new math" is that my son is beating me on his allowance and I can't figure out how!

† † †

People are a lot like chickens and if we had feathers, most of us would peck each other to death.

† † †

We should learn to retire with dignity in the evenings of our lives. No matter how bright its day, even the sun must go down.

† † †

Most folks want something magic, but none of 'em want to pay the magician.

† † †

If postage stamps keep going up, our ZIP will soon be known as ZAP.

† † †

Blood seldom comes from the veins of "Bleeding Hearts."

† † †

Lonesome is being surrounded by people reaching *end* instead of reaching out.

† † †

"Making time pay" is a phrase worth coining.

THE THREAT

Papa woke us 'fore day. The smell of coffee mixed delightfully with the aroma of sourdough biscuits. Mama was getting ready to get off to Monroe.

The corn needed plowing 'n Papa'd said we'd hafta put our shoulder to it.

Soon as The Threat had left with Mama, we commenced to chase the yearling oxen to yoke 'em up and side harrow. We chased those durn critters all over. By 'n by, one of 'em ran so much he just died. We knew Papa wouldn't be pleasured by this 'n he'd probably oblige us with the same. 'Sides, the corn wasn't plowed 'n all.

We were fit to be tied. Then all of a sudden, it struck us. Our cousin was spending a spell at our house 'n he was a big ole splay-footed boy with mud grip feet. We allowed he could pull a mighty load 'long side that off ox.

Soon as we could talk him into saving us from a flogging, we made ready to pin him in the yoke.

Lord-a-mighty, I ain't seen nothing like what happened.

That ox bellered 'n took off dragging him through the barn 'n briars 'n barbed wire 'n all. I'd never seen my cousin so strung out. We chased 'em for more 'n a quarter 'n cornered 'em in some locust sprouts. He was a pitiful, sickly thing standing there almost foundered and puffing like he had a condition. We eased up to unpin him from the yoke, when he walled his eyes and bawled: "Unhitch the other'n— hell, I'll stand."

Well sir, it musta placed a mark on that boy 'cause he never ate nothin' but oats after that . . . and then only out in the barn.

✝   ✝   ✝

A mind in mourning is a grey-matter cloud.

I can trade talk at coffee breaks
or exchange ideas at teas.
But when I sip at cocktail time
someone always swaps my knees!

I "share crop" a garden with the birds. I trade all my strawberries for their morning songs and, after they sing, they pick the fruit and I gather the greens.

† † †

When you are in love with someone who is not in love with you and you are a hundred miles from them, then you are only a hundred miles apart. But if they are in love with you also, then you are two hundred miles apart . . . or even more.

† † †

It's tough growing up, but it's even tougher being a grown-up.

† † †

When I plant things, I don't depend on a green thumb . . . I rely on an "all my knack" system.

† † †

Insurgents who burn a cathedral with wild abandon never realize it takes much less time to fell an oak than to grow one.

† † †

Fat clogs with cholesterol, overloads the heart, loses lovers, and lets people go to waist.

† † †

My uncle uses alcohol only for medicinal purposes and if he doesn't get a drink by five, he's sick!

MATTHEW'S COW

Me 'n Carl 'n Cack had been shelling corn half the morning 'n saving the cobs. We had most a croakersack full when we laid by. We toted 'em 'round to the rainbarrel at the end of the barn 'n dipped out some lardbuckets full of water 'n poked the cobs down in 'em. We had us a cob war comin' up 'n a wet cob was much better'n a dry one for raisin' a blister and truer to the aim.

Carl had to go help Mr. W. J., so it was just me 'n Cack left to make ready for battle 'n soon nobody but me 'cause Cack's Pa came out 'n changed the chores.

I climbed to the top of the old log barn, wedged a bucket of cobs between the notched ends next to the scuttlehole, shinnied cross the pole over the center of the wagon hall, put the second bucketful behind a bale of hay, 'n stuffed some shucks 'round it. I hid two more pailsful, climbed the fence, 'n headed toward the house.

The Davises were having fried chicken by the smell of the air, so I poked 'round their trash and found the heads 'n feet 'n other parts, 'cause I knew where I could catch me a batch of crawdads with this kind of bait.

I got me a ball of twine and tied each part to the separate pieces of string and headed for the creek. I saw Cack back out at the barn 'n whooped at him. He came a runnin'.

Wadn't long 'til we had caught us a washtub of crawdads. Big uns, too.

We put a couple of big buckets of water on the fire 'n dumped two handfuls of salt in the tub of crawdads so they'd purge 'emselves. When the water got to boilin', we poured out the salt water 'n dumped the hot water on top of 'em. Seemed like a mean thing, but God musta known that's what we'd do to clean 'em, 'cause that's the only way I ever heard of. Soon as they all turned red, we started dippin' 'em out and hullin' out their tails 'cause we never did save the heads or claws. By 'n by, we had us a couple of syrup buckets full.

81

We put a black pot of grease on 'n when it boiled, we dumped the tails 'n spuds in it 'n mixed up two quart jars of imitation cherry drink we got from the Raleigh Products man. We ate 'n drank until our stomachs hurt—a good kinda hurt. We laid down on the ground 'n let our crawdads settle. We talked about how we was gonna be rich when we got big 'n we were so busy building us up a business, we didn't even hear the Matthews' old jersey cow 'til she was right on us. She was a hooker and meaner'n old billy be dadgum.

Cack rolled under the wash table where Mama stored the tubs and I lit out on my all fours for the nearest tree, while she hooked at the tubs and my buddy. I swore I'd get that dadburn cow. Later on, after Cack had gone home, I got me a hammer 'n nail, a syrup bucket, and a piece of switch cane 'n started building me a trap for that hooker.

I drove a hole in the center of the bottom of the bucket, put a couple of dabs of water in it, picked up my can of carbide, 'n lit out for the gap down by the lane where that heifer always came up at night.

I had waited until she was within fifty feet of me before I lit the end of my switch cane, 'n dropped some carbide on the water in the bucket 'n jammed the lid on tight. When I struck the match, the cow saw me and eased up to about ten feet of me all walleyed 'n spooked. She lowered her head 'n with a bawl rushed me. I touched the burning cane to the hole in the bucket 'n all hell shook loose. The carbide cannon exploded with such devastation that the fool cow looked like she was up on her hind legs dancing. I was blown over the gate 'n by the time the dust cleared, I saw her runnin' through Springhill Cemetery bellering like a goat caught in a fence. She stayed gone for five days and when she finally came up, she didn't come up the lane. Her milk stayed curdled for three weeks, but she never hooked nobody no more 'n 'specially if you carried a syrup bucket 'n a switch cane.

I believe an individual's rights should be respected as long as he respects the rights of all others.

✝   ✝   ✝

Some pro football players play as if their wives depended on it.

✝   ✝   ✝

I love to cook. More than that, I love for my kids to enjoy what I cook and each one of them go all out to pleasure me by devouring everything in sight.

✝   ✝   ✝

What he does in the long run is the only way you should judge the race of man.

✝   ✝   ✝

Man, the "upright" animal, who has learned
to sing and write and think—
to talk and paint and build houses, cars,
and bombs and carry the world to the brink!

✝   ✝   ✝

A rolling stone may gather no moss, but oh! the sights it sees.

✝   ✝   ✝

Anyone unwilling to earn should not have a choice in charity.

✝   ✝   ✝

Maybe the only reason most fat folks are jolly is they're just trying to laugh it off.

✝   ✝   ✝

In our egotistical way, the tallest man we know is the one who looks up to us.

I sit in solitude, yet I am not alone.
You are here with me as always.

You were my yesterdays,
you will be my tomorrows,
you are my now.

When you smile, I recall every sunrise.
When you cry, I know why it rains.
You make each moment a memory and time a
tender thing.

No small wonder I save a place for you
beside me, if only in my mind.

August 1969

A garage sale is where strangers pay you to haul off your junk.

✝   ✝   ✝

The only thing worse that a "werewolf" is a "was wolf."

✝   ✝   ✝

Even a good year has its week times.

✝   ✝   ✝

The deepest chasm known to man is the human mind. Unexplored regions. Thoughts stored in endless warehouses. Yet few people go beyond the "loading platform." If we tried diligently each moment of every day to place ideas, research, reflections into every corner and crevice of the brain, we could never fill it to the full if we lived a thousand years.

✝   ✝   ✝

All human beings have a price tag and only the pure have not been on the auction block.

WATCH OUT FOR THE SCUTTLE HOLE

I was hopping on one foot toward the house 'cause my carbide cannon had put my left foot to limping. One thing I learned about curing a cow from hooking is never try to hold the cannon down with a bare foot. Soon as I got home, I washed my foot with coal oil and knew that come morning it'd be better. It was worth all the pain though just remembering the look on that heifer's face when I fired the carbide.

I drifted off to sleep wonderin' how far that cow had run before she'd run down.

Morning came with a mockingbird as an alarm clock. I rolled out of the featherbed and commenced to get my chores done, 'cause this was the day we were going to have our corncob war.

When I got to Cack's barn, enough had got there to choose up sides. We were all dressed alike. Everybody had on three-button overalls and was barefoot. You could get a better toe holt if you didn't have on brogans. The morning had woke up hot, so it was a good day for war. Half of us got on the south end and the others got on the other end of the barn and Cack sailed a cob across the top of the hay loft to signal the start. Whush, Whush, Whush, Splat!! A wet cob found its mark. The first blister was earned by John and you coulda heard him holler from the railroad trussle to the crossing, but you had to be a grown man to stand up under a good thrown cob and not moan. We knew old John would stay and fight. Calvin came 'round the barn a-runnin'. He was left-handed and could throw two cobs at a time, one high 'n one low and he ain't never missed nobody. I rolled out of the scuttlehole on the north end of the barn and ran toward the west eave. Old Sid was on my side 'n he was being sorely thumped by the Langford brothers who had him cornered by the wagon. I let fly with a couple of waterlogged cobs that sounded like twin snakes hissing. They found their mark 'n set ole Sid free.

85

He cut through the barn hall while I covered his withdrawal—dustaflyin'—I know he was hit hard 'cause he was catchin' air. I turned and headed for the safety of the scuttlehole but it had been overrun by the invaders. Cack hollered! "Look out for the scuttlehole!" But it was too late to save me. I was knocked off my feet, rolled down to the eave, hit the ground runnin'. I fled to the corn crib with the enemy on my tail, wet cobs buzzing!!

I had two cobs left and when I drew back to throw my first one, I poked it about half way into a red wasp's house with all of 'em home. They had been neutral up 'til then but they made us all retreat. There wasn't nobody that didn't get stung least once, and it sure made you forget where the cobs had hit you.

Both sides retired to the water trough to wash their wounds 'n laugh about who got hit by whom or stung where by what. We ministered our wasp bites with chewing tobacco juice and bluing 'n pumped water on each other's heads 'til we all cooled off.

It would be a marvelous happening if all wars could be settled at the water trough with everyone laughing with and at each other and the only thing buried being a bunch of wet corncobs by nature's great compost pile.

✝   ✝   ✝

It's just as useless to argue with a man who is cocksure he is right as to rassle a grizzly. You come up a loser most the time and very seldom cultivate the friendship of the bear.

✝   ✝   ✝

Let every chore be as enjoyable as whatever you'd rather be doing and it will seem to be completed in half the time.

Don't push love against a wall.
Let it have some room.
Leave it free that it may be
alive to grow and bloom.

Let it orbit the earth,
the stars and Mars and sun.
It will come to you, if true,
and let the rest be done.

I have loved you since yesterever,
since before the earth or time.

And I will go on loving you
'til hell shall change its clime.

To love thy neighbor as thyself is easy to do if he thinks
you're the greatest guy on the block.

✝   ✝   ✝

We should not be embarrassed if we cry in front of our
friends, for no less is it in sharing than a laugh when we are
happy together.

✝   ✝   ✝

Lawyers and liars have as much in common as do politicians and prevaricators.

✝   ✝   ✝

Pathetic politics is a result of an apathetic public.

✝   ✝   ✝

The dreams that come true are usually the ones we have
when we are awake.

JOB DID'T CUSS, EITHER

Percy was a deliberate man. He was short with thick shoulders, and he spoke with just a wee pitch of a lisp, but he never ever used profanity. Percy's wife, Beulah, was his twin physically and usually the first to second his commotions, but she didn't speak with a lisp.

They owned an old Model A Ford, which was second-hand when they first got it and now it looked like a dog's breakfast and was about as ornery on running as a dammed-up ditch. On Thursday, July 26, 1934, Percy walked out to the old car with his first cup of coffee and stood surveying the engine, pondering its fate. Beulah joined him, sipping at her own steaming cup.

"What ya thinkin' 'bout Sugar?" she questioned her husband.

After about three minutes of meditation, he answered.

"Thith ole tar hath got to be tweeted wif a ovahaul."

"Who ya gonna git to do it? Plez?" she asked and answered her own question.

"Nothur, I 'bout to do it mythelf," Percy said with wounded dignity.

Now, he wasn't taking anything away from Plez, because everybody knew he was the best shade tree mechanic in the area, and besides, he could always fall back on Plez if he got in over his head.

The preparations for the overhaul were awesome in their day. Each step was as preponderous as the planning of a pyramid.

The first thing Percy had to do was build a work table and put up a block and tackle to lift out the engine so he could dismantle the motor without losing any parts or something ending up in the wrong place.

He chose a place between two oak trees that would support the hoist and could also be used for legs for the workbench. Next step was to get the old car somewhere in the vicinity of the trees. So, with much deliberation, he pushed and pulled and pshawed for two days, with Beulah bowed up and heaving too, until they got the old "A" up to the area of overhaul.

Only six weeks had passed from when he first made the decision to revive the old Ford. "Well, a man has to make preparations and the hoist and table took two weeks to plan, two weeks to build and two weeks to double check." And, of course, with the pushing, pulling, and pshawing—"a feller just couldn't be too careful in gitting fixed."

The motor support bolts and nuts had long since rusted together and had to be chiseled off, and after busting knuckles for a good two hours, Percy finally worried them off. Next, he disconnected the radiator and radiator hoses, then separated the engine from the clutch housing. Percy was greasy from fingernails to forehead and from armpits to ankle bones. He had gotten this much done and "heck fire" it hadn't taken him but fifteen weeks and three days and that didn't count no Sundays. Well, he might git more done, but each piece had to be looked over a spell to make sure which tooth had to come out. He didn't want to lick his calf but onct.

Beulah had supper hot when he got through scrubbing off with Old Dutch cleanser and Octagon soap. Percy said the blessings and dug into his bowl of crowder peas and cornpone soaked in pot likker.

"How ya comin' long, Sugar?" Beulah asked.

Without answering, he took a bite of the soaked pone and peas, chewing very slowly, then crunched into an onion. Beulah poured him some more tea and replenished the ice in his fruit jar glass.

Percy bit off some more onion, following up with pone and peas, then took a long drag of tea and said: "Purdy fast, I'd thay, if you'th to asth me."

"Well, I did ask, Honey," she replied.

"Purdy fast," Percy said.

Thus ended their conversation for the evening.

Percy got into his flannel night shirt, said his prayers, and crawled quietly into bed. Tomorrow he had some real hard decisions to make 'cause he was gonna pull the engine and maybe take the head off, he just wasn't sure. Morning came announced by the shrill cry of a bluejay. Percy rolled out of bed, put on his overalls, gulped down some breakfast, and made his way out to the point of operation. He had to hurry for Cleet was coming by to pick him up for work by six-thirty. Percy picked up a wrench, put it down, picked up a hammer and pecked at the frame, laid it aside, picked up a pair of pliers, opened them, closed them. It was then, Cleet blew the horn at the end of the lane. "A man just can't git nuthin' done for work," Percy thought.

By the time they got to the field, the crew had already begun work and was busy rolling pipe off a trailer and the welder was cussing up a storm, acting high and mighty. Percy cringed under the profanity, because just any day now God was going to strike that welder with a bolt of lightning and he shore didn't want to be nowhere near. Cleet crawled on his tractor with Percy running along behind him, carrying about seventy pounds of chain. He was Cleet's swamper and he prided himself in being right there when he was needed.

Cleet's job was simple enough. He would position his tractor where the lift extended over the pipe, and Percy's job was to wrap the chain around the pipe and hook it to the lift so it could be raised off the ground. Then a chunk of wood would be placed under the pipe to keep it out of the ditch until the painters could coat it. Percy's chain had a hook on each end and would weigh a good man down, but Percy never let the tractor haul the load. He toted it like Satan holds to sin, gathered in his arms and bellied up to it with the look of a man suffering a double hernia.

If Percy would let his chain be hauled, all he would have to do was loop the chain around the pipe once and hook it to a link, but that wouldn't cut it with him. He never failed to

90

hang one hook on the lift, then wrap the thirty feet of chain around and around the pipe until he could hook the other end on the lift. All in all, it took twenty-nine times longer, but it never varied—hook, wrap, wrap, wrap, hold, hold, hernia.

The Super called for Cleet to bring the tractor down the line and off he buzzed. Percy got him a new holt and bellied up to the chain to wait.

One of the roustabouts remarked how good old Cleet could drive that rig.

Whereupon, after thinking on it, Percy observed, "Yeth, he shore do, but he'th so hard to catch on to anything." Then he leaned into his chain and worked on his hernia some more.

Back home that evening, Percy had to use lights to continue the overhaul and about ten-thirty, he had the engine loose enough to tighten the hoist to lift it up and swing it over on the table, only to discover he had not removed the fuel lines and wiring.

So it would be tomorrow before the reluctant "A" would give up its engine. On Saturday, the head was removed from the block and each bolt, stud, and nut was washed in casin' head gas and placed in individual paper sacks and marked, then deposited in the rumble seat compartment for safe-keeping. Time moved relentlessly on as each piece was scrutinized, sanded, and sacked.

Only five and a-half months had passed since he decided to extend the life of the old motor.

On the next Sunday afternoon, Plez stopped by to look over the progress. He knew Percy wouldn't be working on the Sabbath, but he could kibitz the craftsmanship of a novice. Never in his born days had he ever seen the likes under any shade tree. New rings, new wires, new bushings on everything that needed bushed; each piece gleaming. All Percy had to do now was reassemble the parts, and he was visibly pleased at Plez's praise.

Eight months and seventeen days later, the hoist had re-tightened on the hooks holding the engine. The block painted original red and the head, factory blue. A sight to behold! When the last bolt was secured, new radiator hoses in, and fan belt adjusted, even new brass fuel lines installed—boy, it shore looked good.

Percy spread the hood out like the wings of a large metal bird and wrenched the fasterners down, then lowered the sides. You could see the engine gleaming through the wind slots of the hood.

Beulah remarked: "It's a shame the old body doesn't look as good as that motor."

Percy decided then and there—"That tar ain't gonna move a hair 'til I paint it."

While Percy chipped, sanded, and scrapped, Beulah refurbished the seat covers, head liner, and floor mats. Percy even scraped and painted the wheels back to their original yellow.

One year and two months since "operation overhaul" began, they stood back and observed the gleaming black automobile with the bright yellow wheels.

"Let's crank 'er up and take 'er for a spin, Honey," Beulah purred.

"Nothur, we gonna wait 'til in a mornin' 'n go to Thundy Cool," Percy decided.

Sunday came ruddy-faced and blue-skied. White shirt 'n shined shoes were dug out for church-going. Beulah had on her purple hat and when she climbed into the car, she said something flapperish to Percy, who blushed. Percy climbed in, kinda lifted his arms wing like and flapped them up and down and crowed.

"Man, don' thith tar look dood?" Percy stated the question. The engine started right off and Percy advanced the spark lever and let the motor cluck for him. Then he eased it in reverse and started backing away from the hoist. He was so proud and excited, he didn't notice the guy wire on the light pole and before he could stop, the rear axle had slipped up the cable. The old car teetered for a moment and then flopped over on the driver's side. Beulah was squealing like a stuck pig and tromping all over Percy's head and shoulders getting out of the overturned Ford. She hopped to the ground hollering.

"Get out, Percy, get out, Percy. I smell smoke, get outa there!"

Percy's head popped up through the opening and in no time flat he was clambering over the rear bumpers, wild-eyed and running.

The whole car was engulfed in flames and in less than ten minutes, the auto was a twisted hulk of smouldering steel. Beulah watched Percy walk out toward the barn. She didn't call out or follow. Sometimes a man needs to be alone.

There were tears in Percy's eyes when he opened the cow lot gate. He looked up toward the sky and said—"Thun of a gun."

The devil looked at Percy and said, "Well, I'll be damned!"

It was about nine o'clock Sunday morning, the twenty-first day of September, 1935.

† † †

Nobody has thrown a silver dollar across the Potomac since George Washington 'cause money just doesn't go that far anymore.

† † †

I've been so busy doing business that I've been too busy to do business.

† † †

It's hard to feed a hungry mind if the body is starving.

† † †

The pursuit of happiness is a freedom not franchised solely to the young.

If there is to be a tomorrow
perhaps there is a to'ever way.
Then . . . just maybe . . .
all our yester'nevers could become
to'now
today.

If I could survive for a thousand years
and possess immeasurable worth,
I would rather a pauper be
and live an instant in your near
than to endure forever in the close
of everyone else on earth.

The loss of the "art of conversation" is something we
ought to talk about.

✝   ✝   ✝

We can only measure good news by how bad the last
good news was or bad news by how good the last bad news
was.

✝   ✝   ✝

How can we teach our kids reality today when out of
mouths of babes usually comes an artificial pap?

✝   ✝   ✝

Reach out and touch someone, whether it be by look or
call or physical. When you do, it will make you an extra special someone and, if only for a moment, you will have lived.

✝   ✝   ✝

I would rather give than to receive . . . for it's easier to
give up giving than to give up getting.

94

Enjoy a good day
and charge it to me . . .

The Pause